Cambridge Elements ⁼

Elements in Organization Theory
edited by
Nelson Phillips
Imperial College London
Royston Greenwood
University of Alberta

THE SEARCH FOR THE VIRTUOUS CORPORATION

A Wicked Problem or New Direction for Organization Theory?

Justin O'Brien
University of Sydney

CAMBRIDGE
UNIVERSITY PRESS

CAMBRIDGE
UNIVERSITY PRESS

University Printing House, Cambridge CB2 8BS, United Kingdom

One Liberty Plaza, 20th Floor, New York, NY 10006, USA

477 Williamstown Road, Port Melbourne, VIC 3207, Australia

314–321, 3rd Floor, Plot 3, Splendor Forum, Jasola District Centre, New Delhi – 110025, India

79 Anson Road, #06–04/06, Singapore 079906

Cambridge University Press is part of the University of Cambridge.

It furthers the University's mission by disseminating knowledge in the pursuit of education, learning, and research at the highest international levels of excellence.

www.cambridge.org
Information on this title: www.cambridge.org/9781108969222
DOI: 10.1017/9781108979368

First published 2021

A catalogue record for this publication is available from the British Library.

ISBN 978-1-108-96922-2 Paperback
ISSN 2397-947x (online)
ISSN 2514-3859 (print)

The Search for the Virtuous Corporation

A Wicked Problem or New Direction for Organization Theory?

Elements in Organization Theory

DOI: 10.1017/9781108979368
First published online: September 2021

Justin O'Brien
University of Sydney
Author for correspondence: Justin O'Brien, justin.obrien@sydney.edu.au

Abstract: The corporation is the most complex, adaptive, and resilient model of organizing economic activity in history. In an era of globalization, the transnational corporation holds significant power over society. While its rights are specified through private ordering and choice of jurisdictional home, in the event of conflict of laws, the corporation's duties and responsibilities remain contested. Notwithstanding the argument in institutional economics that all transactions take place within governance and legal frameworks, underpinned by a 'non-calculative social contract', the terms are notoriously difficult to define or enforce. They are made more so if regulatory dynamics preclude litigation to a judicial conclusion. This Element situates the corporation – its culture, governance, responsibility, and accountability – within a broader discourse of duty. In doing so, it addresses the problem of the corporation for society and the corporation's problem in aligning its governance to changing community expectations of obligation.

Keywords: corporate governance, business ethics, organization theory, trust, accountability

ISBNs: 9781108969222 (PB), 9781108979368 (OC)
ISSNs: 2397-947x (online), 2514-3859 (print)

To Stephen and Robert for teaching the true value of professional virtue and in memory of my late brother Brian who has embarked on the ultimate voyage, sailing Into the Mystic

Contents

1 Regulating Conduct and Securing Optimized Outcomes

At the core of organization theory lies the exploration of a trifecta of interlinked factors on the nature of power: identifying its source, measuring its status and consequential capacity to create and maintain hegemony, and evaluating the legitimacy of its operation (Clegg, 2003). Each component is informed by 'constrained optimization' (Nielsen, 2003). Irrespective of theoretical underpinning, each contains an implicit normative agenda. The sustainability of any organization is dependent on ongoing public acquiescence to the corporation's stated core purpose and management's capacity to deliver on it. Nowhere is this more important to society than in the case of the contemporary corporation. The warning signs concerning overweening power, a lack of accountability, and capacity to distort society have animated discourse since the publication of *The Modern Corporation and Private Property* (Berle & Means, 1932) provided legitimacy for the creation of the contemporary regulatory state (Landis, 1938; O'Brien, 2014). Critical questions remain unresolved – stubbornly so. This derives from an ongoing failure to address identified practical, philosophical, and jurisprudential flaws (Mason, 1960, p. 19).

Classic accounts of scientific management position the concept of 'purpose' as central to organizational operations (Barnard, 1968; Chandler, 1977). Social theoretical approaches seek to explain how authority is generated, with an emphasis on identifying differing types of rationalization, and how these interact and compete for influence (Weber, 1958, 1994; Hennis, 1988; Du Guy, 2009). Far from conceiving a single universal logic, Weber (1994, p. 357) doubted whether 'it is in fact true that any ethic in the world could establish substantively identical commandments applicable to all relationships'. An influential review examining the causes, processes, and consequences of organizational misconduct discounted the utility of philosophical explanations on the grounds that there are multiple rational reasons behind the privileging of incommensurable values (Greve, Palmer & Pozner, 2010; see also Ashforth & Anand, 2003; Moore et al, 2006). This approach occludes the primacy of politics in setting the rules of the game, which simultaneously empowers and constrains regulatory capacity and ability. Moreover, the exercise of regulatory discretion has a cascading impact on what cases reach judicial determination.

Political perspectives focus on the exercise of power accrued, with more critical theorists suggesting that consent is manufactured through a complex process of ideational framing (Gramsci, 1971; Haywood, 1994). Recent sociological explanations emphasize the dynamic interaction between rules, principles, and social norms in determining the reflexive logic of practice (Bourdieu, 1990, 1996; Somers & Block, 2014a, 2014b). These rarely link back to how the resulting behaviour derives from preferences already enshrined in legislation (see Hanrahan, 2018). Behavioural accounts, likewise, miss the political. They tend to emphasize that organizational responses to crises are enacted rather than encountered: the result of sense-making derived from previous commitments, actual capability, and perceived expectations (Weick, 1988; Weick, Sutcliffe & Obstfeld, 2005). They suggest that social construction processes bracket behavioural cues and interpretation, transforming moments of crisis into an opportunity to explore organizational adaptability, resilience, or the collapse of authority (Weick, 2009). They do not provide a holistic account of the corporate order.

Each approach provides a fragmentary glimpse at an unresolved and unresolvable problem: how to rebuild trust in the operation and regulation of markets in distrusting times (O'Brien, 2019). It is only through their integration that the corporate order, along with its capacity to adapt to and influence the ecosystem it operates within, comes into clearer view. Mapping this gap is central to strands of regulatory theory that situate the loci of material and ideational power within distinct but overlapping social and physical geographies (Hancher & Moran, 1989; Hood, Rothstein & Baldwin, 2001; O'Brien, 2003, 2007, 2009; Porter & Ronit, 2006). If academic research is to have relevance, it must break free from the permafrost of disciplinary silos and address anew the question of purpose and the metrics by which progress is measured. In sharp contrast to the advice to jettison philosophy (Greve, Palmer & Pozner, 2010), this Element argues for a need to re-engage with it. In seeking to address the problem of the corporation and its influence on society, a speech given by Winston Churchill to the assembled ranks of the Massachusetts Institute of Technology retains potency and relevance:

> No technical knowledge can outweigh the knowledge of the humanities in the gaining of which philosophy and history walk hand in hand. Our inheritance of well-founded slowly conceived codes of honour, morals and manners, the passionate convictions which so many hundreds of millions share together of the principles of freedom and justice, are far more precious to us than anything which scientific discoveries could bestow. ... Human beings and human societies are not structures that are built or machines that are forged. They are plants that grow and must be tended as such. Life is a test and this world a place of trial. (Churchill, 1949)

We would do well to ponder this quotation before continuing. Think what it means to you as a scholar, practitioner, regulator, politician, or member of the public. Then consider to what extent your work and practice are informed by a philosophical anchor. Without it, one is navigating treacherous water without a compass.

1.1 The Point of Purpose

Purpose provides an internal strategic action plan and a normative agenda. Both are encapsulated in corporate mission statements. They signal what interests are to be privileged (or constrained) to optimize determined performance. Internal control mechanisms operate through formal codes of conduct; disciplinary procedures; and risk, governance, and compliance guidelines. These form the baseline from which to evaluate performance against external control criteria. They, in turn, include industry codes of conduct, along with listing, legal, and regulatory licencing requirements (Chiu, 2015). Agreement on a narrowly defined purpose allows for goals to be set, targets met, and return on investment measured. This framing applies to individual corporations, the networks they participate in, and the ecosystems in which they are situated (Shipolov & Gawer, 2020).

Less often accounted for is how the legal community is itself a pivotal policy entrepreneurial class. It mediates access to and control over the coercive powers of government. Increasingly, adjudication of disputes takes place in the shadow of the state. This includes voluntary acquiescence to legally binding arbitration (Porter & Ronit, 2006; Pistor, 2020). It also applies to regulatory reliance on negotiated prosecutions. Despite the high fines, critically, there is rarely an admission of liability. The settlements can privilege the 'façade of enforcement' (Rakoff, 2019). They may represent the triumph of symbolism over substance in the exercise of discretion (Edelman, 1964; O'Brien, 2003, 2007, 2009, 2014). As intimated in the opening paragraphs, although informed by legislation, judicial capacity to provide the precedent necessary to facilitate 'progress' – a critical metric of 'performance' – is limited if the regulator does not seek court guidance or the political establishment proves resistant to strengthening penalties or mandates. The outcome is the same: stasis.

This raises two questions: why is legislation constructed in the way that it is, and whose interests does it serve? At a time of ideological fervour, when what constitutes the truth is contested (Kakutani, 2018) and expertise is devalued (Nichols, 2017), the corporation and its advisors have become key knowledge brokers and, by extension, powerbrokers. Their disproportionate capacity to inform and influence regulatory outcomes raises profound legitimacy concerns. These centre on the interrelationship between political liberty and the corporation in matters that go far beyond the workplace (Clemens, 2009). Seen in this context, corporate power distorts both social welfare and electoral outcomes. Although somewhat colourful, a recent account evokes the dystopia associated with evasion or shrugging, of the kind canvassed by Ayn Rand (1957) – itself the mainstream accompaniment to Hayek (1943). In sharp contrast to freedom, in the United States corporate power has

> produced a kind of Bolshevik dreamland in which a few billionaire hyper-capitalists and libertarian extremists oversee a sizable cadre of professional ideologues and organizers who do the boring, technical and persistent work of radicalizing, training and rewarding, and controlling conservative legislators, policy theorists, media figures, propagandists, administrators, evangelists and judges. This produces a self-sustaining vanguard with real power, and real expertise and a ferocious dedication to victory that increasingly surpasses any allegiance to ethical and civic norms associated with modern democracy. (O'Neill, 2019, p. 91)

The progressive left in the United States has proved no match in terms of organizational power. It has privileged tactical voter mobilization drives over ongoing strategic repositioning of the terms of the debate itself (Winter, 2019). Not surprisingly, it has lost traction. One can see the reason for such pessimism in the defensive positioning of the Democratic Party. Take, for example, Joe Biden's policy address setting out his claim to take on Donald Trump in the 2020 United States presidential election:

> Democracies – paralysed by hyper-partisanship, hobbled by corruption, weighed down by extreme inequality – are having a harder time delivering for their people. Trust in institutions is down. Fear of the Other is up. And the international system that the United States so carefully constructed is coming apart at the seams. (Biden, 2020)

Stating the problem does not solve it. For Biden (2020), 'combatting corruption is a core national security and democratic responsibility'. He argues for the need to establish a Commission on Federal Ethics. He advocates constitutional reform to reduce the influence of private money in steering (or distorting) electoral outcomes. Irrespective of the merit of Biden's proposal, the election was fought under the current rules. This necessitates paying considered attention to how the corporation acts, individually and through networks and ecosystems. More importantly, it necessitates an evaluation of how the rules of the game are set and interpreted through the communities of practice that act as custodians of the law. The stakes have rarely been higher in peacetime.

Declining trust in our governmental institutions reflects their incapacity to tame negative forces unleashed by the financialization of the economy (Davis, 2009; van der Zwan, 2014). The application of regulatory authority is dependent on the ability to marshal ongoing political support. This is a delicate process, as demonstrated by the enfeeblement of the Securities and Exchange Commission (SEC) in the United States, following the passage of Sarbanes-Oxley. Sarbanes-Oxley is legislation passed in 2002 to inculcate a corporate conscience in the aftermath of the implosion of Enron and WorldCom amid a welter of scandals over the efficacy of the audit process and conflicts of interest over the provision of analyst research ratings (O'Brien, 2003, 2007).

The reliance on 'gate-keepers' failed at all levels of oversight, across myriad professions and those aspiring to professional status. Even as scholars were communicating the results of the conflict of interest scandals at the turn of the millennium (Coffee, 2006), legal engineering facilitated an expansion of the logic of financialization (O'Brien, 2009; MacNeil & O'Brien, 2010; McBarnet, 2010). The impact on the real economy were, as expected, devastating (Fligstein & Goldstein, 2015). At a broader and more pernicious level, commodification had deleterious effects on social cohesion across most of the liberal order. Short-termism became corrosive.

There is nothing unethical, for example, about securitization – the primary method for shifting the quality and quantum of risk off bank balance sheets. What is up for debate is the efficacy of internal and external controls and how risk was conceived, operationalized, and communicated to the wider market. A mechanistic reliance on disclosure allowed those in charge of product design and disclosure to abdicate responsibility for the toxic products sold into the market because the risks were cited but ignored (O'Brien, 2013). All of this was perfectly legal and informed by an ideational view of the world, which was precisely that.

The shareholder-value model of corporate law dominates the epoch of investor capitalism (Jensen & Meckling, 1976). Echoing public discourse, the law and economics tradition suggested social responsibility was, at best, a distraction (Easterbrook & Fischel, 1989). It proclaimed as late as 2001 that, for corporate law, we had reached 'the end of history' (Hansmann & Kraackman, 2001). Leaving aside the hubris (made manifest by the dot-com collapse, emerging questions on the failure to manage conflicts of interest, and the erosion of professional restraint in the accounting profession), the only certainty offered by this research program is that it was a hostage to fortune. It was only a matter of time before it would be falsified. The length of time it has taken demonstrates the ideational power of the concept, not its veracity, as the maestro of central banking was to concede in an excruciating testimony to Congress (Greenspan 2008a, 2008b).

What was presented as economically rational was, it transpired, nothing more than an ideological conceit, a problem first identified by Polanyi (1944) and given recent data-driven confirmation by Piketty (2020). Economists, it appears, can learn – even if belatedly. The investor-capital model lost legitimacy precisely because it failed to embed restraint or constraint. A narrow focus on property rights excluded from consideration the needs of essential stakeholder interest groups, including suppliers, clients, customers, and employees. In sharp contrast to the promise of the new institutional economics (Williamson, 2000, p. 597), the 'non-calculative social contract' said to underpin legal and governance frameworks that guide individual transactions was unenforced and unenforceable.

1.2 Creative Destruction and Destructive Creation

Capitalism thrives through disruption, which facilitates innovation and a reallocation of capital to those nimble enough to adapt to changing contingencies. Creative destruction may well be the driving dynamic of capitalism, as Schumpeter (1943) famously suggested. These very forces can, however, unleash destructive creation. Those who unthinkingly use the aphorism to lionize innovation do well to remember the prescient warning that the 'stock market is a poor substitute for the Holy Grail' (Schumpeter, 1943, p. 119). The alchemy mesmerized not only economists but proponents of 'material sociology', who thought little of the long-term consequences, or potential consequences, of what they were observing on the production lines of Wall Street and the City of London (MacKenzie, 2009). There is little point having access if one does not understand or call out the possibilities of unethical conduct, a problem not confined to neophyte sociologists (Agius et al, 2010).

The rise of the technology sector shows similar problematic traits to banking. Shareholder activism has been powerless to stop the inexorable rise of new monopolies. These cannibalize existing industries for content on platforms for which they subsequently decry any responsibility. These same titans are governed through ownership structures that differentiate voting and economic interest shares. The violation of best-practice corporate governance guidelines is worn as a badge of honour. It also means the existing owners are impervious to effective market oversight. It is indicative that one of the most innovative products made by Apple is, arguably, its tax strategy, which through transfer pricing has significantly eroded tax revenue across the markets in which it derives its profits.

Apple is by no means alone. At the time of writing, Facebook, the world's largest social media corporation, is fighting an Internal Revenue Service adjudication that prior to its flotation the corporation failed to book more than $9 billion in profits owed to the United States by using a subsidiary in Ireland in a scheme that crossed the line between legal avoidance and illegal evasion

(Murphy, 2020). Facebook accepts that its systems were messy while contending, somewhat blithely, there was no guarantee that its internationalization strategy would have been successful. It sounds suspiciously like an each-way bet within a gamed casino. For both corporations, legal engineering was required to facilitate the transfer pricing model.

Meanwhile, economies of scale allow for an ever-deepening concentration of power. Innovation is often bought in through the acquisition of start-ups from entrepreneurs whose ambition is to invent, bring to market, and then sell to the oligopolies, thereby further embedding power and further distorting competitive markets (Cohen, 2017). Facebook is valued at $640 billion; its four other major actors – Alphabet, Amazon, Apple, and Microsoft – have market capitalisations of more than $5.6 trillion. Together, these five firms account for 20 per cent of the value of all S&P 500 shares. The total fines and penalties paid, or proposed, amount to less than 1 per cent of these corporations' market values (*The Economist*, 2020). We are asked to rely on protestations that we can trust these unelected and unaccountable titans to facilitate social change. Outsourcing the resolution to existential crises to unelected, unaccountable corporate entities with a vested interest in the outcome is not, however, advisable. If the essence of the problem is to ensure constrained optimization, then allowing a doubling down on the investment is unwise.

This is manifest in the rise and fall of WeWork, once the world's largest commercial real-estate developer (Edgecliffe-Johnson & Platt, 2020). Erroneously described as a 'start-up', WeWork's rapid expansion earned it the moniker of a 'unicorn'. Its calibrated messaging made it a faith company with an initial public offering (IPO) awaited with excitable interest because it had disrupted the real-estate market (e.g. Leclercq-Vandelannoitte & Isaac, 2016; see, however, Aronoff, 2017). It was only when the company released its IPO that the hubris and governance problems showed that it was not a unicorn worth pursuing. WeWork was a classic property play, based on little more than bombast and greed.

As we enter a new epoch of industrial development in which the nature of work itself has changed (Sennett, 1998), there is renewed interest in mapping the normative determinants of 'stakeholder capitalism' (Bowie & Freeman, 1992; Freeman et al, 2018). This is not in itself uncontroversial. Constraining unchecked managerial discretion was critical to the normative foundational logic of investor capitalism in the first place (Friedman, 1970). The shareholder-value proposition had the benefit of parsimony. It gave corporations a clearly defined purpose. The problem is that in so doing, transactional imperatives replaced relational ones. Value was measured solely in short-term pecuniary terms. The skewing of compensation towards stock-market performance created a self-reinforcing dynamic detrimental to the long-term interests of the corporation itself (Braithwaite, 2020). The problem extends far beyond the finance and technology sectors.

The crisis engulfing Boeing, for example, centres on the accusation that the corporation privileged profit over safety in the redesign of its 737 Max aircraft. Two of the redesigned aircraft crashed in 2019, forcing the grounding of the entire fleet at a huge financial and reputational cost to the corporation and devastating personal loss for the families of the bereaved (MacGillis, 2019). One of those onboard the Ethiopian Air 737 that crashed outside Addis Ababa in March 2019 was the great-niece of Ralph Nadar, the activist who in the 1970s brought attention to the social cost of the elevation of profit over safety in the automobile industry (Nadar, Green & Seligman, 1976). Now the Nadar family are asking the same questions of a sector thought immune to such forces.

How did it come to this? Financial engineering proved much more brittle than its industrial counterpart; so too was the integration of computer programming into the engineering design process, a dismal reality facing not only Boeing but breathless supporters of disruptive technologies, including artificial intelligence and machine-based learning. It is by no means certain that a moral compass can be designed and implemented through algorithms in order to integrate earnings smoothing with a 'preoccupation with failure' (Weick & Sutcliffe, 2015). These may turn out to be incommensurable activities.

The critical function of any given governance framework is to ensure that the organization, network, or ecosystem can survive and adapt to contingency (Morgan, 1986). To ensure this operates according to principles of informed consent necessitates ongoing vigilance. It is unwise to rely on a mechanistic application of process. Such an approach may offer a rich description but has little predictive power (Du Guy & Vikkelsø, 2014). Moreover, it can occlude an actual understanding of what is really taking place (Munir, 2011), as the painful story of material sociology demonstrates only too clearly. If stated purpose is no longer in alignment with actual practice, the cooperative system fractures and with it comes the potential loss of internal and external legitimacy (Greenwood & Miller, 2010). Here again is evidence of the consequences of myopia. After all, we have long known that 'if we are to improve the functioning of our organizations from within, and to gain control of them, then we must understand the power relationships that surround and infuse them' (Mintzberg, 1983, pp. 1–2).

Corporate power derives from concrete legal foundations. It is built on a regulatory system that is no longer fit for purpose (O'Brien, 2019). Complexity is built into the system through the legal coding of capital itself (Pistor, 2020; Hanrahan, 2018). Law is the unseen source of power and domination (Weber, 1958; Lukes, 1974; Mann, 1986; Poggi, 2001). It is essential to unpack this in order to understand the power of the corporation in and over society. This task raises profound practical and theoretical questions. Curiously, these are not explicitly addressed enough in organizational theory (Clegg, 2003; Davis & Zald, 2009). As a coding device, the corporation and its interrelationship with the democratic process is also a 'wicked problem' (Rittel & Webber, 1973).

A wicked problem, by definition, is unresolved and unresolvable. The concept has been susceptible to stretching by overuse to describe problems that are difficult but not insurmountable (Peters, 2017; Termeer, Dewulf & Bresbroek, 2019; Noordegraff, 2019). In other domains, the insertion of additional restrictive criteria generate 'super-wicked' problems – namely (a) that time is running out, (b) no central authority exists to take leadership, (c) those charged with change are themselves responsible for the problem, and (d) the future is so heavily discounted that the political gains of immediate action are less valuable (Levin, Cashore & Auld, 2012). The influence of the corporation and what to do about it is a paradigmatic example of a super-wicked problem.

Corporate rights give unparalleled access to the coercive power of the state. Concomitant duties and responsibilities to society, however, remain contested and contestable. The negative impact is most pronounced within liberal democracies. Understanding and taming the corporation is critical to the future of organizational studies and its credibility as a discipline (Davis & Zald, 2009). The corporate form and its legal ordering remain critical, if under-explored. If law is the source of power, its practitioners are the conduits of change (Edelman, 2007; Edelman & Talesh, 2011). It is the empire of corporate governance and its regulation that need to be recalibrated (O'Brien, 2019). It is time to bring the corporate order into the centre of organizational analysis through a review of the substantive concerns of corporate law and securities regulation. All too often the emphasis on enabling conditions over defined purpose short-changes societal welfare, generating profit through unseen government direction (Somers & Block, 2014b).

1.3 Bringing the Corporate Order Back In

The primary goal of social science research is to confirm, modify, or falsify theory (Popper, 1959). Falsification comes from determining whether abstract theoretical premises match empirical evidence. Without developing and testing theory, we risk the confines of normal science becoming so restrictive that the knowledge generated is irrelevant. The problem with paradigms is that, once established, they can become citadels to defend (Kuhn, 1962). While often presented as a useful framing device, a paradigm can become a prison (Fuller, 2003). This is something that those working within the confines of normal science can find a threat and threatening (Davis & Zald, 2009). It is indicative of the myopia that this generates, that Kuhn is often presented as a libertarian and Popper a rigid authoritarian defender of past practice (Fuller, 2003). This distorts Popper's warning in the closing paragraphs of his most famous work, *The Open Society and Its Enemies*:

> If we think that history progresses, or that we are bound to progress, then we commit the same mistake as those who believe that history has a meaning that can be discovered in it and need not be given to it. For to progress is to move towards some kind of end, towards an end which exists for us as human beings. . . . And we shall do it much better as we become more fully aware of the fact that progress rests with us, with our watchfulness, with our efforts, with the clarity of our conception of our ends, and with the realism of their choice. Instead of posing as prophets we must become the makers of our fate. We must learn to do things as well as we can, and to look out for mistakes. And when we have dropped the idea that the history of power will be our judge, when we have given up worrying whether or not history will judge us, then one day perhaps we may succeed in getting power under control. In this way, we may even justify history, in our turn. It badly needs a justification. (Popper, 1984, pp. 279–80)

By revisiting the classics, we can identify the strength and weakness of past theoretical reflection. All too often, these canonical works are cited rather than understood. The classics serve six instrumental and strategic purposes. They are touchstones, prompt development tasks, signal theoretical foundations, and provide lineage. They also serve a routine science function, providing a framework for resolving conceptual puzzles. Finally, they provide a ritual function, meaning they provide an intellectual home (Stinchcombe, 1982). As Thornton (2009, p. 23) points out, this strategy opens productive lines of inquiry (citing Homans, 1964; Baron & Bielby, 1980; Skocpol, 1985; Friedland & Alford, 1991; Thornton, 1999). This Element focuses primarily on the fifth function. It evaluates how distinct theoretical perspectives within and beyond organizational studies address (or fail to reach) the core of the corporation problem.

Clemens (2009) has argued provocatively that it is pointless to look to the classics. She notes that neither Hayek (1943) nor Polanyi (1944) conceives of the corporation as a distinct actor, with the capacity to distort both markets and polities. She mourns the lack of a defining text, arguing that 'some of the greatest theorists of the 1930s and 1940s did not simply ignore the problem but actively marginalized it', with the result that 'the problem of the large corporation and liberalism was a classic waiting to happen' (Clemens, 2009,

p. 536). In large measure, however, this is understandable. Hayek, Polanyi, Popper, and Schumpeter were writing at a time of existential crisis. It was by no means clear whether democracy could or would survive. The subsequent Cold War facilitated ongoing distraction. This is not to say that ideational contestation was unobserved or deemed unimportant.

The problem identified by Clemens has long been central to legal scholarship (Berle, 1931, 1960; Dodd, 1932; Mason, 1960; Blair & Stout, 1999; Hansmann & Kraakman, 2001; Greenfield, 2006). Clemens acknowledges the importance of *The Modern Corporation and Private Property* (1932), arguably the most influential book on corporate law, but heavily discounts the political context in which it was written. There is a strong disconnect between the emphasis in the final chapter of *The Modern Corporation* that shareholder action has the capacity to resolve an agency problem caused by the separation of ownership and control and the preceding text. The entire book warned that the corporate form was already out of control (see Bratton & Wachter, 2008). Berle (1960) himself was to concede that law had generated a system that left only stewardship as a restraining force, the position adopted by his sparring opponent Dodd (1932) in the pages of the *Harvard Law Review*. Both the problem of the corporation and the corporation problem are a function of law. It is only through law that it can be resolved, if only temporarily and, then, only until the regulatory space shifts once again. While Clemens (2009, p. 545) is correct in positing that 'contemporary debates [within organizational studies] foreground the pseudo market created by public policies while paying little attention to the organizations that populate them', the same cannot be said for corporate law scholarship and regulatory theory (Landis, 1938).

The fundamental point of this Element is to introduce to the field analysis of how the code of capital is created, adapts, and sustains its legitimacy. This has a direct practical application. The rise of populism across the globe is now threatening the stability of legal orders (Deenan, 2018; Piketty, 2018, 2020). In late 2019, the influential World Economic Forum (WEF) released the Davos Manifesto. It links corporate purpose to active stewardship in driving progress towards fulfilling the United Nations Sustainable Development Goals (O'Brien, 2020). This constraining of shareholder value is further embedded by the WEF's active support for the Organization for Economic Cooperation and Development (OECD) campaign to deliver global tax reform. The OECD's Base Erosion and Profit-Shifting initiative is critical to minimizing corporate tax avoidance strategies that skirt close to illegal tax evasion. The active support of the WEF marks a decisive moment in the debate over the parameters of corporate social responsibility (Mayer, 2019). It re-anchors the corporation to the nation-state and to the communities in which it operates (not where it is domiciled for tax and legal arbitrage reasons). It highlights the importance of managing a social licence to operate, taking responsibility for corporate actions in ways that transcend legal obligation. The unresolved question is: will it work?

It is in this regard that the failure of past initiatives gives pause for thought. Statements of regret are insufficient. Trust in the corporation needs to be warranted, not merely stated. Compliance must be substantive, not technical. Here, well-functioning regulatory processes can provide the framework to facilitate debate and deliver substantive change (Landis, 1938). These require skills in legal and regulatory gamesmanship. To achieve sustainable transformative outcomes, it is necessary to change the sense-making of the legal community. Current practice can provide comfort that conduct can be legal, if potentially unethical. It may facilitate transacting around the spirit of legislative and regulatory intent, while closing avenues for final judicial determination, often with implicit regulatory support, the result of ideational capture, timidity, or realism. Ascertaining which variable dominates is critical to evaluating legitimacy.

1.4 The Corporation and the Limits of Enacted Law

Between 1972 and 1974, Christopher Stone assembled a team at the University of Southern California to examine the systemic factors driving corporate malfeasance. These factors were then analyzed by a group of social scientists. In an early example of interdisciplinary research, the group included a systems analyst, an organizational studies specialist, an industrial sociologist, and a psychoanalyst. The results were startling. *Where the Law Ends: The Social Control of Corporate Behavior* (1975) retains its verve and relevance. In line with legal scholars and political scientists (Berle, 1931; Dodd, 1932; Mason, 1960), and mindful of the concentration of corporate power (Nader, Green & Seligman, 1976, pp. 20–21), the identified problem for Stone was clear. It was pressing, long ignored, and inherently dangerous to stability if unaddressed: 'Corporations have long since become, for better or worse, the most effective "private" forces to do widespread good and widespread harm. For this reason, to solve society's problems is, in no small measure, to come to grips with the corporation problem. But what is "the corporation problem," and how is it to be dealt with?' (Stone, 1975, p. xii).

For Stone, the problem lies in how the legal framework conceives the corporation as an individual. Neither statutes nor regulators nor markets hold the coercive or rehabilitative tools to address effectively corporate non-compliance with social norms. None has the capacity to identify malfeasance and misfeasance, hold the corporation itself accountable, or inculcate a program of moral development. Indeed, when conceiving of a corporate conscience, 'it is not readily apparent where we would begin – much less what we would be talking about' (Stone, 1975, p. 35). Law's efficacy depends on

> its consistency with and reinforcement from the other vectors – the organization's rules for advancement and reward, its customs, conventions, and morals. If the law is too much at odds with these other forces, its threats will make the employees more careful to cover their tracks before it makes them alter their institutionally supportive behaviour. (Stone, 1975, p. 67)

The innovation advanced by Stone is the proposal to extract concrete information about how responsibility is conceived in operational terms. This is achieved by identifying and evaluating the actual 'cognitive processes [deployed within corporations]' (Stone, 1975, p. 116). This suggests the need to 'focus on the *processes of corporate decision-making*, at least as a supplement to the traditional strategies that largely await upon the corporate *acts* [emphasis in the original]' (Stone, 1975, p. 121). What Stone is emphasizing here is a lost administrative ideal (Landis, 1938). The ideal was already in disarray when Landis (1960) revisited the fate of his progeny on behalf of President-elect John F. Kennedy. It was to enter a near-fatal decline.

The dynamics of regulation take place within a contested and contestable terrain. We omit the political dimension at our peril. While the New Deal is often presented as a coherent architectural design, it reflected multitudinous and conflicting ideas that ranged from corporatism to the promotion of self-regulation (O'Brien, 2014). A ceasefire was brokered with the Supreme Court upholding the constitutionality of the *Public Utility Holding Company Act* (1937) and the passage of the *Administrative Procedure Act* (1946), but the hostility of business and sections of the political firmament towards the regulatory state never weakened, nor did a cohesive framing develop, as the following account of the conflicts in the 1970s makes clear:

> The imprecision of the ideology that justifies the existence of administrative agencies reflects the [ongoing] basic ambivalence of our society towards the process of regulation. When a nation cannot find the intellectual wherewithal to formulate a coherent ideology on an issue as fundamental to its values as the balance to be struck between a free market and state regulation, such regulation as it does authorize will always be subject to philosophic as well as pragmatic question. (Freedman, 1975, p. 1054)

The United States and, by extension, the global legal order continues to wrestle with this wicked problem. The enduring nature of the corporation problem is reflected in contemporary debate. How do governance, culture, and conduct interact? How intrusive should the role of regulators be, and on what basis is this justified? If the corporation is best conceived as an individual, how does one balance rights, duties, and responsibilities? From a normative perspective, the possibility of restraint becomes embedded institutionally the more the corporation thinks of its duties and responsibilities across multiple domains, including those as a citizen, producer, resource manager, investment vehicle, neighbour, competitor, and social designer. Just as importantly, it is essential to put in place metrics to 'identify a whole range of underlying attitudes and forces and proceed to identify the particular sorts of undesired corporate behaviour that constitute their symptoms' (Stone, 1975, p. 236). In so doing, we come closer to understanding the operating reality of lived cultures, not only within the corporation as an organization but the organization of socioeconomic and political life.

It has recently been argued that the United States has 'lived through the era of corporatism, the era of transactionalism, and the economists' hour. The intellectual marketplace awaits a fresh approach to the structuring of work and the good society' (Mallaby, 2019). This adds to the concern raised by Clemens (2009). As with Clemens, however, the role of law, and the related question of its legitimacy, has been ignored. The answer to the corporation problem and the problem of the corporation depends on what we choose to see in philosophical as well as material terms (Murdoch, 1960). There is no doubt of the need to broker a corporate social licence to operate (Gurria, 2017). To be effective, it must be capable of ensuring the integration of profit and purpose, and aligned to the moral development of the corporation itself (Vinten, 1990; Rossouw & van Vurren, 2003; Gao & Zhang, 2006; Hess, 2008; Rahim & Idowu, 2015). This necessitates a deconstruction of how white-collar crime is conceived as part of a wider philosophical exploration of the determinants of corporate duty and obligation. As will become clear, the utility of the journey lies in discovering how cultures can and often do distort by normalizing deviance. The irresponsibility associated with systemic unethical, if not necessarily illegal, conduct highlights the gap between societal expectation and corporate practice. A major part of the problem of the corporation is that many in the corporate sector do not believe there is a problem.

More than a century ago, a muckraking journalist fulminated that 'the modern high-powered dealer of woe wears immaculate linen, carries a silk hat and a lighted cigar, sins with a serene soul, leagues or months from the evil he causes' (Ross, 1907, p. 10). It was and remains an arresting description. It forces reflection on the nature of corporate crime and how violations of the law are perceived within and between different groups in society. Much of what occurred in the GFC was perfectly legal, if ethically irresponsible (O'Brien,

2009, 2013, 2019; McBarnet, 2010). Without reflection on the impact of action or inaction on others, there is little room to utilize the leveraging power of guilt and shame. Practice, including the failure to detect misfeasance, has long been justified as the price of doing business (Sutherland, 1939). As such, it can privilege neutralization strategies (Stadler & Benson, 2012; Klenowski, 2012). This occurs either as ex ante excuse or ex post rationalization. Misconduct can become normalized through opportunity (Benson & Simpson, 2015), convenience (Gottschalk, 2017), or insouciance if the conduct complained of is technically legal or the result of 'creative compliance' (McBarnet & Whelan, 1999). If shame and guilt are defined by conduct that departs from community expectations, how can their restraining power be harnessed? These are by no means simple questions. They cut, however, to the core of how responsibility and accountability can be defined, measured, and evaluated in a corporate context. Here, evidence from Australia has potential utility for illustrating how comprehensive mapping can provide a solution.

The Australian *Royal Commission into Misconduct in the Banking, Superannuation and Financial Services Industry* (2019, pp. 8–9) called for a corporate commitment to six core normative values: 'obey the law; do not mislead or deceive; act fairly; provide services that are fit for purpose; deliver services with reasonable care and skill; and when acting for another, act in the best interest of that other'. These principles are a start. They are only a start. What does 'act fairly' mean? When it suggests that financial services must be 'fit for purpose', what purpose is being referred to? What constitutes the parameters of 'reasonable'? By what criteria should we measure 'best interest'? How an institution conceives of its purpose is essential to holding it accountable. It is true that equity offers ways in which to evaluate these competing considerations. Utility is weakened, however, if through the privileging of regulatory discretion, the rules of the game deal out judicial intervention.

The identification and explanation of conduct cannot occur without an evaluation of underpinning culture. It is through culture that social norms are propagated, embedded, legitimated, and sustained. Deconstructing the dynamics of culture is a task that has exasperated scholars and critics alike (e.g., Elliot, 1948; Steiner, 1971; Eagleton, 2016). Cultures can be repressive as well as enlightening. They are as much instruments of control and hegemony as bulwarks of civilization. Notwithstanding the difficulties of defining causal reasons, we are witnessing the disintegration of the rules, principles, and social norms binding society. This has pressing socioeconomic and political implications that go beyond the corporation. They can only be resolved, as Stone made clear, in conjunction with it. How, then, does one reconnect law, morality, and community expectation? Putting aside its complexity, without addressing this challenge it will be impossible to transcend 'the cultural contradictions of capitalism' (Bell, 1976). Which is, after all, the epitome of wickedness in policy terms.

With the growing atomization of society, it is even more difficult to articulate and (self-)police with precision supererogatory 'hyper-norms', which are consistent with 'integrative social contracts'. (Donaldson & Dunfee, 1999, p. 50). The emphasis on 'hyper-norms' in procedural, structural, and substantive forms mirrors the analysis put forward by the Australian Royal Commission. It believed that the task can be left to a simplification of law (Royal Commission, 2019, pp. 494–6). It is unlikely to be sufficient. As an influential background paper pointed out, legislative complexity and regulatory delineation are by no means accidental:

> The result is legislation that is labyrinthine. The definitions that mark out the regulatory perimeter are lengthy and often the rules themselves are highly specific and detailed; these are often made in response to relentless industry pressure on governments and regulators to supply black-letter prescriptive rules and guidelines that allow compliance risk to be managed internally by firms using a check-box approach. (Hanrahan, 2018, pp. 11–12)

Legitimacy and renewed authority can only come from the integration of formal philosophical reasoning into corporate policy and practice. It cannot be left to expediency or legislative instruments, flawed in design or application. The approach canvassed here is consistent with six core criteria of deliberative governance (Dryzck, 2012). It provides a mechanism to address the concerns over corporate power voiced by democratic theorists such as Dahl (1957) and Lindblum (1977) and their organizational studies counterparts (Clemens, 2009; Davis & Zald, 2009). First, the deliberation must take place in a public space that encourages active engagement. Second, it must be empowered to inform and influence the trajectory of public debate. Third, it should provide an effective transmission mechanism facilitating the exchange of information. Fourth, accountability is guaranteed by the integrity of the process itself, which has a mandate to subject reform initiatives to ongoing empirical and conceptual testing. Fifth, through the co-production of knowledge within and across sectors, it should facilitate meta-deliberation. Sixth, it should aim to guide industry towards socially beneficial and sustainable outcomes. This cannot occur without the articulation of promises and warranted assurance that those promises have meaning.

One useful starting point, and one which is explored throughout this Element, is the synthesis offered by the late philosopher Derek Parfit. He argued that an act is moral if it is 'universally willable [categorical], socially optimific [consequential] and not unreasonably objected to [through the calculated application of the intellectual virtues and habituated through practice]' (Parfit, 2011, p. 321). While the reasoning is highly abstract, its logic has direct application to business practice. Of even greater significance, it addresses a vacuum at the core of the liberal project: 'the point about liberal freedom is that it is non-redemptive. It is not visionary and does not seek to transform anyone or anything' (Ignatieff, 2017, p. 191).

Without the countervailing force of equality of opportunity to provide security and common purpose, liberalism, and freedom to contract offer scant comfort in a deeply uncertain world (Piketty, 2018, 2020). Moreover, if the law is something that can be transacted around with impunity, the result is institutional corruption (Lessig, 2018; Miller, 2017). The search for a solution to ethical misfeasance is complicated by the language we use to describe our choices. Is it a consequence of commitment to subjective 'values' or objective 'virtue'? Does anything lie in the distinction? As it happens, everything pivots on the linguistic turn. The question is whether those values are in themselves informed by ethical obligation or nothing more than instruments of social coercion (Nietzsche, 2013).

1.5 Distinguishing Virtue from Values

Trust is a social phenomenon. Its capacity to act as a social glue depends on belief in the trustworthiness of another (North, 1981, 1990). It is, therefore, essential to address the question of authenticity with philosophical rigour. Aristotle (2004b, p. 145) held that authenticity requires the integration of 'contemplative and calculative intellect'. Appetition, meaning a craving for a specific purpose, can only have virtuous character if the desire is calculated according to this contemplative understanding. It necessitates acceptance of a broader purpose than one engineered for self-interest alone. For Aristotle, the end-point of happiness is the flourishing of human existence. This goal is to be achieved primarily through political deliberation: 'The end of political science is the highest good; and the chief concern of this science is to endow the citizens with certain qualities, namely virtue and the readiness to do fine things' (Aristotle, 2004b, p. 21).

When the virtue of the consequential purpose – happiness – disappears, the ethical underpinnings risk being unanchored. An authentic corporate life, there-fore, requires an active balancing of conflicting imperatives. The lived life must reflect a warranted commitment to genuinely held inner beliefs. This choice must be made purposively. Engagement must be real. It must be built on empathy. It must be empirically grounded. This is not necessarily difficult. It informs debate on the purpose of political economy, consistent with Adam Smith's theory of moral sentiments: 'every passion of which the mind of man is susceptible, the emotions of the bystander always correspond to what, by bringing the case home to himself, he imagines should be the sentiments of the sufferer' (Smith, 2006, pp. 4–5). Authenticity, in a virtuous sense, therefore, requires an alignment of thoughts, words, and actions.

Seen from this perspective, social progress pivots on 'a communitarian conception of economic morality that defines correct ethical behaviour through the device of a hypothetical social contract emphasizing the moral understanding of living members of economic systems and organizations' (Donaldson & Dunfee, 1999, p. 86). This necessarily imposes significant limitations on corporate freedom in exchange for security and stability, a point endorsed by leading ethicists as 'to have any kind of liveable society some choices have to be restricted, some authorities have to be respected, and some individual responsibility has to be assumed. The issue should always be which choices, which authorities and responsibilities, and at what cost' (Taylor, 2007, p. 479).

The distinction between 'values' and 'virtues' encapsulates the difficulty in legal and policy terms. This is, as noted previously, more than a problem of linguistics. Addressing the lexicological difference is, however, essential. Building on the work of George Orwell, Benson (2018) argues that the corruption of language leads inevitably to the corruption of thought. One of the words most susceptible to such misappropriation is 'values'. It is often presented as functionally equivalent to 'virtue'. For Benson, parallel usage is false. It leads to inadvertent or deliberate confusion. To buttress the case, he cites the Canadian philosopher George Grant: 'No-one can tell me what a value is. It seems to me an obscuring morality used when the idea of purpose has been destroyed' (Benson, 2018, p. 11).

To clear up this confusion, it is essential to revisit the academy of ancient Athens. Here again is evidence that the classics need to be interpreted, not merely cited. Aristotle (2004b, p. 31) argued that 'intellectual virtue owes both its inception and its growth chiefly to instruction, and for this reason needs time and experience. Moral goodness on the other hand, is the result of habit.' Critical to living a virtuous life is knowledge and commitment. This presupposes three criteria: '(1) if he knows what he is doing, (2) if he chooses it and chooses it for its own sake, and (3) if he does it from a fixed and permanent disposition' (Aristotle, 2004b, p. 37). To rely on an underpinning principle or value is both commonplace and misplaced. An examined life is a difficult one, honoured more often in the breach.

> This is not, however, the course that most people follow: they have recourse
> to their principle, and imagine that they are being philosophical and that in
> this way they will become serious-minded – behaving rather like invalids

who listen carefully to their doctor, but carry out none of his instructions. Just as the bodies of the latter will get no benefit from such treatment, so the souls of the former will get none from philosophy. (Aristotle 2004b, p. 38)

In deriving a working definition Aristotle (2004b, p. 42) holds that 'virtue is a purposive disposition, lying in a mean that is relative to us and determined by a rational principle, and by that which a prudent person would use to determine it. . . . Thus, from the point of view of its essence and the definition of its real nature, virtue is a mean; but in respect of what is right and best, it is an extreme.' As such, it is a decision best made through deliberation over the means to an end rather than an end in itself, with virtue giving both the instrumental means and outcome. As Popper (1984, p. 280) was to later endorse, 'it lies in our power, and similarly so does vice, because where it is in our power to act, it is also in our power not to act, and where we can refuse we can also comply' (Aristotle 2004b, p. 61).

Speaking specifically about justice as a virtue, Aristotle draws a distinction between lawful or fair, by which he means equitable. 'In justice is summed up the whole of virtue' (Aristotle, 2004b, p. 115). Fairness is a necessary corollary and this 'is the essential nature of equity; it is a rectification of law in so far as law is defective in its generality' (Aristotle, 2004b, p. 141). The problem for the corporation is that these defects have not been tested in law, in part because of the structure of law itself, which deals out the judiciary through reliance on regulatory discretion. In examining the causes of distrust and providing mechanisms to address them within an overarching meta-theoretical foundation, we anchor industry more firmly to the societies in which it operates. The battle is fought increasingly on the contested terrain of value and values, seen most notably by a change in the trajectory of the OECD, with its embrace of 'inclusive capitalism' (Carney, 2014, 2015, 2018). In 2019 the OECD Director of Financial and Enterprise Affairs, Greg Medcraft, set out an ambitious agenda at the annual northern spring meetings of the International Monetary Fund and World Bank in Washington, DC. He endorsed the link between 'value' and 'values' through a renewed social contract.

> While business is pursuing *value*, governments are pursuing *values* as the basis for policymaking. That is to say, the normative decisions we have made as a society about what kind of world we want to live in, and what outcomes our laws and markets should deliver. The good news is that, in terms of outcomes, there is little difference between business value and social values –. because business needs to align its behaviour to what society expects. (Medcraft, 2019)

This Element begs to differ. There are huge differences between values, which one's are to be privileged, and the entire relationship between value and virtue.

If we are to articulate a new theory of the corporation that balances rights, duties, and responsibilities within a framework that has global application, predicating the discussion on values is foolhardy. It is where the law ends that the journey to redemption begins. In so doing, we truly climb the mountain of understanding what matters (Parfit, 2011).

2 Sympathy, Empathy, and the Pursuit of Reason

It is perhaps not surprising given the emphasis by Weber (1958) on the import-ance of the Protestant ethic to the spirit of capitalism that the theoretical justification for its paradigmatic emergence should come from the university on the hill in the west end of Glasgow. The quintessential industrial city, Glasgow is the intellectual birthplace of John Calvin and the puritanical postu-lates that inform his vision of purpose. Self-restraint and hard work would provide opportunity, which, if reinvested rather than spent in displays of ostentation, would unify the needs of God and man. Profit itself was to become a form of prayer and a signal of redemption. As such, capital provided the bridge to unify the needs of the City of God and the City of Man. Values were reduced to a material value, the price of which was to be determined in the marketplace.

The compromise was neither new nor without risk. It can be traced back to the fourth century. 'The philosophers have engaged in a great deal of complicated debate about the supreme ends of good and evil; and by concentrating their attention on this question they have tried to discover what it is that makes a man happy' (St Augustine, 2003, p. 843). For the theologian, the answer was clear. Whether happiness derived from the soul, the body, or both, it required the pursuit of an end to be desired for its own sake. Thus 'eternal life is the Supreme Good, and eternal death the Supreme Evil, and that to achieve the one and escape the other, we must live rightly' (St Augustine, 2003, p. 852). Security, stability, and happiness derive from defining what 'rightly' means - a definition that changes according to the means of production (and religious doctrine). To retain currency, it must not lose other-regarding properties. Here one returns to the question of contractual bargaining.

One influential answer of how to reconcile the spatial and spiritual worlds was posited by Adam Smith. Smith laboured as a professor of moral philosophy at the University of Glasgow. He is most renowned for a sardonic metaphor. Transformed into reified dogma – not law – he noted how an 'invisible hand' guided economies, with utility maximization of Hobbesian appetites a proxy for socially beneficial outcomes (Rothschild, 1994; see also Collins, 1999). In the process, Smith became arguably one of the most misunderstood philosophers of economic thought. He remains so.

The Wealth of Nations (1776) cannot and should not be read without reference to Smith's earlier book *The Theory of Moral Sentiments* (1759). The latter connects to the philosophical literature on virtue that date backs to Aristotle (2004a), with a lineage traceable through Seneca to St Augustine and on to Hobbes. To paraphrase Hobbes, the 'warres on want' cannot be won, or even negotiated to a ceasefire, without first determining what constitutes the conscionability of the term. The contemporary value of Hobbes, as with the Smith of *The Theory of Moral Sentiments*, lies not in establishing immutable social norms. Instead, it is in finding innovative ways to legitimate them. In so doing, they have the capacity to fire up possibilities for constant renewal (Bicchieri, 2016). This requires, in turn, parsing further our existential distinction: a society guided by values is not necessarily one informed by virtue.

Recognizing this distinction is essential to understanding the choices facing the contemporary nation-state. If the conscionability of social and commercial contracts alike is to be preserved, each must be understood not just in black letter law form but in active consideration with the positive reinforcing dynamics of social norms and the societal expectations on which they are based. We often forget that in Grecian and Roman times, philosophy was as much a practical as a theoretical matter. The leading Stoic philosopher Seneca provided the compass with which to navigate through such treacherous waters.

> Philosophy is not an occupation of popular nature, nor is it pursued for the sake of self-advertisement. Its concern is not with words, but with facts. . . . It moulds and builds the personality, orders one's life, regulates one's conduct, shows one what one should do and what one should leave undone, sits at the helm and keeps one on the correct course as one is tossed about in perilous seas. Without it no one can lead a life free of fear or worry. Every hour of the day countless situations arise that call for advice, and for that advice we have to look to philosophy. (Seneca, 2004, pp. 64–5)

The same logic applies to the operation of regulatory policy. To understand why, we need to delve more deeply into the interaction between legal and moral philosophy, its application to corporate identity, and how the regulatory state responded.

2.1 The Siren Call of Chrematistic Logic

Short-term thinking, or what Aristotle termed *chrematistic* logic, is as prevalent in political as well as economic affairs (Daly & Cobb, 1994, pp. 138–41). What is new is a growing sense of despair, described memorably by one leading social theorist as the necessity to accept that 'true courage is to admit that the light at the end of the tunnel is probably the headlight of another train approaching us from the opposite direction' (Žižek, 2017, p. xii). It is a provocative but altogether too bleak assessment. We are at an interchange. A shift in track can avert a looming catastrophe. Time, however, is running out. Over-reliance on technical solutions to normative problems enhances the resilience of the existing (failed) global regulatory system (O'Brien, 2019). From this perspective, systemic financial misconduct is not the result of a failure of a culture. Instead, it is the washout from a specific culture's very success. These crises, intensifying in intensity, cannot be understood without excavating the political firmament and identifying the ideational flaws driving the system (Žižek, 2019).

To address the malaise, one must debate anew the meaning of duty and purpose, in corporate and regulatory as well as philosophical and jurisprudential terms. One must remain cognizant throughout that these instruments need sharpening. Years of neglect, hubris, myopia, and arrogance have combined to dull our intellectual senses of the possible and weaken our resolve to address the rise of populism (Muller, 2016). But make no mistake. A start must be made, a point that unifies political theorists from across the spectrum (e.g., Ignatieff, 2017, pp. 82–3; Žižek, 2019, p. 22).

The OECD has cautioned against 'superficial changes to avoid upheaval of the order that works so well for some. ... The truth is this won't work. We are beyond quick fixes to address the discontent of the masses' (Gurria, 2017). In June 2019, the Business Roundtable in the United States made a decisive shift away from short-term profit maximization. In a pledge signed by more than 180 of the largest corporations in the United States, the Roundtable privileged renounced fealty to shareholder value. The influential asset manager BlackRock wrote to all corporations in which it invests, demanding a balance between purpose and profit (Fink, 2019). The message is clear. Environmental, social, and governance (ESG) reporting matters. They matter profoundly. It is in this regard that the Davos Manifesto offers such potential (O'Brien, 2020). Taken together, the regulatory, industry, and corporate decisions suggest the possibility of a fundamental shift in tack to avoid catastrophe.

More effective, more responsible, and more accountable risk-management strategies have become a business necessity. Buffeted from all sides, governmental inaction is providing an accelerant to a veritable bonfire of the vanities. Reliance on existing systems of internal control that vest responsibility at individual business units, overseen by largely ignored risk and compliance procedures verified by internal and external audit, do not work. The false assurance is draining confidence on a global scale. Trust remains in short supply. Technical compliance trumps substantive adherence. Stated commitment to high ethical standards is not and cannot be warranted. Deterrence is defective.

Accountability and responsibility are diminished. Conduct risk remains out of control.

Theorizing on the corporation necessitates sustained investigation of the ideational roots of argumentation. This allows for falsification. It may be sufficient in academic terms. It does not address a deeper problem that has implications far beyond the corporation. What was termed the art of rhetoric in ancient Greece (Aristotle, 2004a) has been regenerated through hermeneutics (Gadamer, 1976). Rhetoric, properly understood, is a branch of philosophy. It is not an exercise in sophistry. This insight is critical to the impact of hermeneutics on intellectual thought.

Hermeneutics holds that interpretation is not just a meaning; it is grounded in a whole set of background practices. As such it is inextricably linked to socioeconomic and political framing and the uses to which it is placed (Gadamer, 1976, p. 376). Seen in this context, hermeneutic evacuation of contingency is antithetical to the self-imposed restrictions of normal science. In much the same way that originalist readings of constitutional law can prohibit changes in social norms, ahistorical readings of core theoretical texts subjugate change to uncompromising fealty to an imagined world. The normative myopia imposed by elevation of a temporary mandate to permanency may preclude the effective search for solutions, a problem we have already identified with the end of history thesis in corporate law (Hansmann & Kraakman, 2001).

Hermeneutical evaluation also helps clarify the arena in which intellectual fencing over shareholder primacy occurs. Shareholder primacy derives its theoretical insights from the application of agency theory (Jensen & Meckling, 1976; Fama & Jensen, 1983). It resurrected a transactional approach to the firm, its governance, and its obligations. What Stout (2007) termed 'the myth of shareholder value' achieved infallible status within the sub-disciplines of law and economics (e.g., Easterbrook & Fischel, 1989; Hannsmann & Kraakman, 2001). The communitarian alternative privileged in the corporate social responsibility literature (e.g., Daly & Cobb, 1994; Donaldson & Dunfee, 1999) reinforced a counter-offensive within corporate law (Blair & Stout, 1999). Neither achieved sufficient traction to shift discourse.

The shareholder-value paradigm is breaking down as the result of the intellectual recognition of intrinsic ideological failure (Mayer, 2019), intergovernmental questioning of its political unacceptability (Carney, 2015, 2017, 2018; Gurria, 2017), and asset managers paying significantly more attention to environment, social, and governance reporting (Fink, 2019). As Mayer (2019) makes clear, disillusion on the streets is mirrored by a dawning reality within the academy that something fundamental is askance. From the perspective of hermeneutic analysis, the key question is: why it has taken so long to answer? After all, even before neo-liberalism shattered the post-war consensus, it was clear that that rise of the modern corporation 'and attending circumstances have confronted us with a long series of questions concerning rights and duties, privileges and immunities, responsibility and authority, that political and legal philosophy have yet to assimilate' (Mason, 1960, p. 19). Part of the problem is a lack of intellectual ambition.

Interpretative studies focus primarily on both content and the context of how the social world is constructed. They do not necessarily seek to change it (Klein & Myers, 1999, p. 69; Walsham, 1993, pp. 4–5). They contribute to a deeper understanding of an objective reality (that is subjectively experienced). The researcher operates on a spectrum from neutral – in the sense of academic non-alignment – to using the data to build iteratively a case for theory extension or calibration (Walsham, 2006, p. 321). This recognizes the importance of a critical point: interpretation cannot be divorced from latent assumptions. Seen in this context, hermeneutic excavation of legislation and judicial outcomes is a circular endeavour undertaken within the set boundaries (or principles) that constitute the parameters of research (Klein & Myers, 1999). It is designed to ensure and assure 'authenticity, plausibility, and criticality' (Walsham, 2006, pp. 325–6). There is no guarantee of accuracy, however, beyond the terms of the paradigm itself (Stahl, 2004, p. 3).

Here again, one sees the dangers of the approach taken by proponents of Actor Network Theory, such as how financial trading floors construct economic agents (e.g., MacKenzie, 2009). The study does not comment on the normative implications of their actions, or how their actions were predetermined. This is a dangerous slope to head down without intellectual crampons. This is particularly appropriate to the study of finance, where the economically rational is itself a political construction and derives, as we have seen, from a misreading of Adam Smith's *The Theory of Moral Sentiments*. How this came about is critical to developing a revised theory of the corporation capable of reducing social contestation and the existential crisis caused by the collapse of trust. One cannot evaluate performance without a foundational purpose to act as a benchmark. What that exact purpose should be remains a matter of contention. The interpretative method can generate concrete information about how institutional change is operating and the efficacy of cultural change agents. It may guide data collection and thematic coding and ensure data-theory linkage from the outset. Through in-depth case studies, for example, dialogue with informants within ethical boundaries may lead to the discovery of pre-existing hidden meaning, including that of the researcher herself (Stahl, 2004, p. 2). The need for caution, however, is evidenced by a 2010 conference organized by

MacKenzie. It focused on the question: does the sociology of finance have alpha? This reinforces the value of critical theory. It is even more vital today in an age informed by anxiety and distrust over corporate purpose and perceived regulatory complicity because as Heidegger's most famous student remarked, 'neither oppression nor exploitation as such is ever the main cause of resentment: wealth without visible function is much more intolerable because nobody can understand why it should be tolerated' (Arendt, 2017, p. 5). Moreover, the strict dichotomy between interpretivist and critical theory is itself open to challenge (Walsham, 2006, p. 321). Although distinct the difference is arguably one of placement on a continuum (Myers & Klein, 2011). Both puncture the positivist position that universal laws order the social world, suggesting that approaching research from a neutral perspective is 'politically impossible and socially undesirable' (Agger, 1991, p. 106).

From roots explaining the failure of the Marxist project, powerful lens – including those of 'hegemony', 'wars of position', and 'wars of manoeuvre' pioneered by Antonio Gramsci have been deployed in political regulatory analysis. Likewise, deep ethnographic analyses informed by empirical evidence, such as those conducted by Pierre Bourdieu (1990, 1996), have also exposed and delineated the hidden multiple sources of cultural and economic power and their interaction. Likewise, the work by Foucault (1982) on the archaeology of knowledge and the political and legal construction of punishment and morality (Foucault, 1982) has challenged cornerstone liberal ideals of linear progression and situated them within contested and contestable arenas. It is indicative, for example, that Bourdieu was the Director of Studies at the Institute for Advanced Studies in Paris, itself part of the elite system he critiqued and was responsible for propagating. Foucault occupied a similar position as Head of Philosophy at the Collège de France. Gramsci alone was to languish in a prison cell.

What the work of each scholar shows is how the rules of any social interaction are constructed. The close observational method that informs *The State Nobility* (Bourdieu, 1996), along with the conception of *habitus*, or field, first outlined in *The Logic of Practice* (Bourdieu, 1990), has proved exceptionally influential in socio-legal studies and regulatory theory (Hancher & Moran, 1989; Hood, Rothstein & Baldwin, 2001; Braithwaite, 2013). None of these authors could be conceived of as having the revolutionary impulses so commonly ascribed to critical scholars. Each operated within the mainstream, deploying hermeneutics as a drill bit to understand how regulatory dynamics actually operate and how law was constructed, an endeavour which has proved much more enlightening (to forgive the pun) than that presented in the positivist account, which suggests law can be separated from social norms, and its application takes place solely in an omnipresent judicial setting. The relationship between law and politics, the state, market, and society, is both symbiotic and inherently unstable. Critical too is the role of eminent law firms in the two central jurisdictions, London, and New York, where the code of capital is created. Revolutions and revolutionaries come from unlikely places.

2.2 Resetting the Board

The interplay between regulatory, political, and corporate 'fields' is critical to ascertaining the nature and operation of power (DiMaggio & Powell, 1983). In mapping these distinct social and political geographies (Hood, Rothstein & Baldwin, 2001), the researcher can contextualize how best practice mutates into 'soft law' with applicability across national and international domains (Porter & Ronit, 2006; Edelman, 2007). In the process, we reach a deeper, more realistic understanding of the social determinants, restraints, and opportunities associated with regulatory performance. The social is indeed a messy world, not suited to the parsimony of universal laws and rational decisions. There is a critical difference between 'law on the books' (Pound, 1910) and 'law in action' (Halperin, 2011). Notwithstanding pleas by the Australian *Royal Commission into Misconduct in the Banking, Superannuation and Financial Services Industry* (2019, p. 434), for simplification, legislative complexity is inbuilt by design. A similar situation pertains in the United States. Legislation such as *the Wall Street Reform and Investor Protection Act* (Sarbanes-Oxley) (2002) ceded to the SEC responsibility to ascertain and design rules and then subject them to a complex note and comment procedure (O'Brien, 2003). This was then itself subject to repeated legal challenges on cost-benefit analysis grounds. *The Wall Street Reform and Consumer Protection Act* (Dodd-Frank) (2009) suffered a similar fate (Fisch, 2013). As should now be clear, enforcement constraints and the choice to litigate come at the end of the process. They are largely predetermined by political factors. They shape future outcomes.

Critical theory facilitates an analysis of how and why this has occurred. It provides a map to navigate the process. Crucially, it provides a framework for building more effective solutions. As currently constituted, enforcement strategies are unlikely to satisfy public perception of law as a moral standard (Habermas, 1996). For Habermas (1996), operational social context drives the legitimacy of law. Building on his earlier theory of communicative action (Habermas, 1981), this focus on the integration of law and norms fuses rationality with metaphysics, or more accurately post-metaphysics. It turns the transcendental into a question of ongoing deliberative discourse.

The bridge linking facticity and validity in Habermas's terms is built from ethical reflection on contested and quintessentially wicked problems. Whether sustainable corporate governance and reform necessitate other-regarding corporate purpose than maximizing shareholder value continues to animate progressive legal scholarship (Ireland, 2000; Stout, 2007; O'Brien, 2019). The critical interpretative approach outlined previously highlights the way in which these challenges can be addressed. It forms the basis of a new program of learning that can power theoretical advances in both law and organizational studies. Take, for example, the dominant regulatory theory of 'responsive regulation' (Ayres & Braithwaite, 1992).

From the perspective of this analysis advanced here, key core questions need to be addressed before one can evaluate the effectiveness of the theory. First, does it help or impede regulatory agencies engineer more beneficial societal outcomes, the critical aim of the administrative process? Second, does it facilitate regulatory capture, rendering it untenable on ethical, practical, and institutional grounds? Third, does it privilege the elevation of the symbolic over the substantive in political and regulatory calculation? Fourth, can it be any longer justified to address the non-calculative social contract that binds society together, identified as a critical but ignored dimension of trust within institutional economics? Finally, is the normative change essential to manage and regulate corporate morality in alignment with societal expectation? Empirical reality suggests the theory is lacking.

The current system of corporate governance and financial regulation shows just how difficult it is to break through ideational permafrost (Rose, 2011) and how technical compliance but ethical derogation is institutionalized. These dynamics must be interpreted, contextualized, and critiqued to make a meaningful contribution to the theory and practice of the corporation and its regulation. Theory must be adapted, as Landis (1960) did in his report to John F. Kennedy, opening in the process new ways of interpreting his masterpiece (Landis, 1938). Likewise, to their credit, both Braithwaite (2013) and Streeck (2016), on whom the former so heavily relied, have recognized and publicly accepted their failure. The same cannot be said of many others. The problem with moving elephants in small spaces is that they tend to break things.

3 Ethics and Risk

Applied ethics in an organizational sense, properly understood, is a means to an end. It is, or should be, a demonstration through evidence of the veracity, falsification, or need for modification of a single or interlinked theoretical construct (Popper, 1984, p. 280). The focus in business contexts, however, is much more defensive. If the problem is pronounced in the academy, it has reached crisis proportions in the business world with which it necessarily interacts (Weick, 2009) but all too often seeks to emulate (Gurria, 2017). So, what can or should be done? It is in this context that the contemporary pluralist approach of Derek Parfit comes into its own, as a diagnostic, palliative, and curative tool.

As we have seen, for Parfit an act is moral if it fulfils three criteria. It must be 'universally willable [categorical], socially optimific [utilitarian majoritarian preference relating to pleasure or its avoidance] and not unreasonably objected to [satisfying Aristotelean requirements that both the act and the reasons for it satisfy intellectual and physical virtues]' (Parfit, 2011, p. 321). This highly abstract approach, if operationalized, can capture most of the dilemmas faced in the business world if linked to the enunciation of broader foundational concepts: justice, non-injury, fidelity, reparation, beneficence, self-improvement, gratitude, and liberty. To this list, more recently, has been added obligations of manner or respectfulness of others (Ross, 1930; Audi, 2004). These are all capable of being monitored if the risk-management system is constructed to actively think (Stone, 1975) and, more crucially, see (Murdoch, 1999, p. 37). In summary, we need to move from an emphasis on process to how and why decisions are made, and whether they are grounded in subjective values or objective virtue. As stated at the outset, this cannot be done without a philosophical anchor. To fully understand why this is necessary requires us to return to Aristotle's distinction between character and intellectual virtues, the latter of which provides the skeletal operating framework to determine the former. Such virtues distinguish between contemplative thinking about invariable first principles and calculative deliberation about what can be subject to compromise, without sacrificing an irreducible element: 'Choice necessarily involves not only intellect and thought, but a certain moral state; for good conduct and its contrary necessarily involve thought and character. But no process is set going by mere thought – only by purposive and practical thought, for it is this that originates productive thought' (Aristotle, 2004b, p. 146).

As a consequence, 'it is virtue that makes the choice correct; but the carrying out of all the natural stages of action with a view to that chosen is a matter not for virtue but for a different faculty' (Aristotle, 2004b, p. 163) – that of cleverness. So, for example, cleverness in pursuit of any given appetition can only have true value if virtuous in its end objective, 'thus it is evident that one cannot be prudent without being good' (Aristotle, 2004b, p. 164). As succinctly restated for contemporary organizational purposes 'to act virtuously ... is to act from inclination formed by the cultivation of the virtues' (MacIntyre, 1984, p. 149).

This necessitates a specification and an evaluation of what those ends are (e.g., the overriding good of the community), itself the result of substantive rational deliberation (Popper, 1984, p. 280). The problem to be overcome is not only one of institutional amnesia but 'isomorphism'. This represents an ever-narrowing range of policy options mandated by a model that drives its legitimacy with rudimentary compliance with black-letter law and bureaucratic oversight (coercive), consistency with best-practice formulations (mimetic), or the need for professional sign-off (normative) within the totality of actors in a given organizational field (DiMaggio & Powell, 1983). To be transformative, we have to address profound power imbalances within that field, an idea that dates back to Landis (1938, 1960) and Edelman (1964). Both scholars assessed how the game was played within the rules. I suggest the time has come to recalibrate the rules themselves to change the process of sense-making itself (Weick, 1988). It is a fruitful change in direction.

3.1 What We Look for Determines What We See

Philosopher Iris Murdoch (1999, p. 28) once commented that 'moral concepts set up an entirely different world from the world envisaged by science and logic (not empirical facts and a moving will within which moral concepts move but a different world)'. These universal and unchanging concepts reflect a deepening of self-knowledge that is proactively used to 'express the idea of a just and loving gaze directed upon an individual reality' (Murdoch, 1999, p. 34). Action has value if it comes from 'within a world I can see', which in turn necessitates the exercise of 'moral imagination and moral effort' (Murdoch, 1999, p. 37). The task for both the individual and the institution alike is to establish 'true vision' to explain 'good conduct' and develop 'rich and fertile conceptual schemes which help us reflect upon and understand the nature of moral progress and moral failure' (Murdoch, 1999, p. 45).

Recognition of the importance and originality of Murdoch's contribution has waned in recent years. The perceptiveness has sharpened in an age informed with scepticism about the limits of reason. For Murdoch, the problem of isomorphism is one that afflicts contemporary philosophy itself, where 'a smart set of concepts may be a most efficient instrument of corruption because . . . we are anxiety-ridden animals. Our minds are continually active, fabricating an anxious, usually self-pre-occupied, often falsifying veil which partially conceals the world' (Murdoch, 1999, p. 82).

The politics of financial regulation is a perfect example of that process in action, aided by the endogeneity of its creation and legitimation at both a national and international level. Here one detects an unwillingness to 'see' in Murdochian terms. The lifting of scales was acknowledged in the initial political response to the 2008 financial crisis. The then British Prime Minister openly canvassed 'whether we need a better economic and social contract to reflect the global responsibilities of financial institutions to society' (Brown, 2009). He sought to rescue the Enlightenment from postmodernism and emphasized that for Smith, 'the moral system encompassed the economic system, generating the responsible virtues of industry, honesty, and reliability, and the stable associations in which we accept our responsibilities each to the other – habits of co-operation and trust, the moral sense upon which the market depended' (Brown, 2008, p. 12). In so doing, he was rejecting the foundations of neo-liberalism. His US counterpart Barack Obama went further:

> Markets are not an unalloyed force for either good or for ill. In many ways, our financial system reflects us. In the aggregate of countless independent decisions, we see the potential for creativity – and the potential for abuse. We see the capacity for innovations that make our economy stronger – and for innovations that exploit our economy's weaknesses. We are called upon to put in place those reforms that allow our best qualities to flourish – while keeping those worst traits in check. We're called upon to recognize that the free market is the most powerful generative force for our prosperity – but it is not a free license to ignore the consequences of our actions. (Obama, 2009)

These priorities waned as the process of policy design and implementation privileged an incremental reactive approach. It elevated the politics of symbolism (Edelman, 1964). Nowhere is this more apparent than in the identification of risk and the delineation of what constitutes prudential governance, a question that must take into account not only a specific act but the rationale and justification for it, as both an exercise of free will and moral choice.

Policymakers and practitioners across the world have now acknowledged that there is a pressing need for the development of a regulatory and corporate architecture based on principles of integrity. What remains unclear is what this nebulous concept means in practice and how to rank competing, potentially incommensurable, interpretations of what constitutes appropriate behaviour (O'Brien, 2010, 2019). Can one say, for example, that acting within the confines of the law shows integrity? This cannot be a satisfactory answer, given the ethical void experienced in both fascist and totalitarian societies, each governed by legal (if morally repugnant) frameworks.

It is equally unsatisfactory to root integrity lexicographically in the application of consistent behaviour. Consistently engaging in deceptive and misleading practice may demonstrate 'wholeness' or 'completeness,' but it cannot be a constituent of integrity. Integrity therefore requires of us not only duty (that is, compliance with the law, along with consistent and coherent actions) but also principles that contribute to (and do not erode) social welfare (that is, treating people, suppliers, and stakeholders with fairness and respect). Seen in this context, enhancing integrity through higher standards of business ethics is a question of organizational design (O'Brien, 2010, 2019). The aim, in short, is to give substance to what constitutes – or should constitute – appropriate principles of aspiration for the corporate order. Even if one views malfeasance from the less demanding utilitarian perspective, the consequential impact – unintended, to be sure – makes both the activity itself and the underpinning regulatory framework equally ethically suspect. Here it is essential to differentiate between the product and the clearly inappropriate uses to which it was put to work.

From an ethical perspective, it is a weak defence for chief executive officers to claim ignorance of either how these products were structured or how unstable the expansion of alchemistic engineering had made individual banks and the broader financial system. It is now recognized, for example, that the originate-distribute-relocate model of financial engineering significantly emaciated corporate responsibility precisely because it distanced institutional actors at every stage of the process from the consequences of their actions. Likewise, given the huge social and economic cost, it is insufficient for policymakers merely to profess shock at the irresponsibility of banks, insurance companies, and ratings agencies. The failure to calculate the risks and design or recalibrate restraining mechanisms at the corporate, regulatory, and political levels grossly exacerbated the externalities borne by the wider society.

We chose not to see. We now require a synthesis between an appreciation of context, the need for virtuous behaviour, and the importance of deontological rules and consequential principles of best practice within an overarching framework that is not subverted by compartmentalised responsibilities. The policy problem is not the relative importance of virtue but whether it can be rendered operational in a systematic, dynamic, and responsive way, with specific benefits to business and society itself. Accountability is, therefore, as noted previously, a design question at both corporate and regulatory levels, which, to be effective, needs to be mutually reinforcing and capable of dynamically addressing the calculative, social, and normative reasons for behaving in a more (or less) ethically responsible manner.

Rules need to work 'hand in glove' with principles within an interlocking system of incentives and disincentives. In some areas, compliance with rules might be more important than alignment with principles. On the other hand, for some problems in other areas – for example, potential conflicts of interest – the emphasis might need to be on principles in the context of verifiable procedural requirements, such as an internal but independent mechanism for determination of any conflict of interest. In other areas, such as disclosure requirements, principles and rules might both need to be met. More generally, principles may require ongoing testing to ensure consistency and coherence in terms of application. How to ensure that rules and principles mutually reinforce one another – rather than compete with one another – is central to regulatory effectiveness.

Strong moral and ethical codes are required to ensure economic viability (North, 1981, p. 47). Sustainable reform necessitates examining which factors contribute to the reinforcement or degradation of social norms. Despite rhetorical commitment to enhance integrity, many of the chosen policy options remain firmly within the existing technical realm, relying on traditional regulatory tools such as enhanced disclosure, literacy programs, and attempts to distinguish between sophisticated and unsophisticated investors. Each proved inadequate in the search for greater (or, more accurately, effective) accountability. Moreover, the issue of what constitutes appropriate levels of disclosure, transparency, and accountability, even within these narrow conceptions, not only remains unresolved. These terms are also subject to intense contestation. Given the fact that markets can be and often are inefficient, effectiveness necessitates dynamic and responsive regulatory guidelines, using the entire suite of enforcement mechanisms, ranging from command and control, through enforced self-regulation, to industry designed and policed codes of conduct. All must be subject to judicial review. We cannot say we have not been warned (e.g., Rakoff, 2019; Royal Commission, 2019). In fact, the warning long predates this. The problem is that we have not paid attention to it.

3.2 Law as Culture

By building on a foundation of common *stated* virtues, an agonistic understanding of what constitutes the problematic core is generated from which deviation lowers reputational standing and access. This framework can only be sustained through an interlocking dissemination network comprising and reinforcing formal and informal nodes. The resulting synthesis has three key practical and normative advantages. First, it reduces real and artificial incommensurability problems between participants in the regulatory conversation (irrespective of whether they have been accorded formal surveillance authority). Second, it reduces the retreat to legal formalism, de-escalates confrontation, and contributes to behavioural modification across the regulatory matrix. Third, by clarifying accountability responsibilities, it offers greater certainty for corporations and the market in which they are nested, thus facilitating investment flows. It provides a more meaningful baseline from which to measure and evaluate subsequent regulatory and corporate performance. It is therefore essential to recalibrate the theory and practice of regulation to incorporate a much more substantive normative component.

In the event of a catastrophe (political, social, economic, or natural), it is rational to reduce one's trust to ever more localized communities. Paradoxically, given the speed and spatial breadth of the Internet, in a virtual world, everything is local. Withdrawal of generalized trust acts as a social filter, echo chamber, and breeding ground for conspiracy theory creation and dissemination. The combination reduces confidence in the competence, benevolence, and integrity of more distant bureaucracies, corporate or political. The return to higher levels of trust can only occur if localized perception of the trustworthiness of institutions increases.

The means of production and dissemination of that trust are necessarily culturally specific. They are also dependent on how compromises are negotiated or imposed. This can take the form of a deliberative exercise that can be either expansive and purposive in meaning or structured to reduce contestation (Luhmann, 1979). At a preliminary level, it is essential to determine where *law as culture* sits within this rubric. While it can be studied in isolation, law is intrinsic to holistic conceptions of risk (Smircich, 1983; Mather, 2013; Pistor, 2020). Subcultures exercise power through both formal and informal mechanisms (Lumineau & Schilke, 2018), both of which are centred on ideational imperatives.

One must be cognizant that normative problems cannot be fixed by technical measures alone, especially when, as in the case of corporate lawyers, those normative settings are themselves socially constructed and largely unexamined. Failure to account for this may lure one into a false sense of security, embedding and legitimating cultures that deliberately occlude risk identification and reporting (Davies & Zhivitskaya, 2018). The gap between outward presentation and emotional core drivers of actual practice may remain (Mitroff & Pearson, 1993; Admati, 2017). While we may choose not to see or move metaphorical elephants, we cannot deny their presence and risk. Credible negotiation and resolution cannot be reduced to crisis-management public relations designed for a geographically or culturally distant headquarters (Weaver, 2001). The existence of formal control systems that contain elements of command, control, coercion, and calculation does not in itself guarantee that any will be used or believed in. Even within corporate headquarters, the emphasis on formal codes as a guarantee of actual compliance can signal little more than moral blindness. The formal controls may demonstrate a lack of pre-existing trust and may through their introduction create or intensify distrust. We remain a long way from safe harbour. In large measure, this is a consequence of mistrust in operational definitions of trust in action.

The duality between confidence that one's vulnerability will not be exploited, and the willingness to take that risk defines trust in action across all disciplines and practices (Rousseau et al, 1998). The trust literature also supports the contention by Stone (1975) that hope has to be accompanied by meaningful action if it is to be sustained (Brion et al, 2018). Trust, once broken, is hard but not impossible to rebuild. Suspicion and fear of being duped are heightened. The quest for self-preservation of dignity and self-worth makes one less willing to take that risk. Given social and group identification, trust can only be maintained through fealty to an albeit amorphous and exceptionally fragile social contract.

This is consistent with the 'narrow corridor' argument put forward by Acemoglu and Robinson (2019). This is difficult to achieve within any community, corporate or political. Order through a coercive Leviathan, however, is the antithesis of the modern liberal state. So too is libertarian faith in the 'freedom to contract' model – hence the 'shackled Leviathan' offers more stable foundations. Responsiveness to public concern can and often does rebuild faith. Prohibitions of slavery, the ending of child labour, extension of the suffrage of women, and the passage of anti-discrimination laws mirror how law reflects, if imperfectly, changing community consensus. Moreover, through judicial or quasi-judicial evaluation, change is capable of direct observation. In so doing, the change can enhance shared belief in the trustworthiness of institutional structures to uphold common ideals. In these circumstances, the withdrawal of trust is itself an instrument of power (Karsgaard et al, 2018). Exercising this power requires exquisite timing to break free from the constraints of passivity, control, and the politics of drift.

3.3 Culture as Desire or Responsibility?

'Desire scoops out a hollow in humanity, overshadowing presence with absence and spurring us beyond the given to whatever eludes our grasp. In this sense, it can be seen as the very dynamic of civilised existence', noted a prominent critical social theorist (Eagleton, 2016, p. 26). For Eagleton, desire itself has no moral compass and is directionless; as such, 'it signifies a flaw at the very heart of our fulfilment, an errancy of our being, a homelessness of the spirit'. By any reckoning, this is also a bleak view of progress. It does highlight that, left to our own devices, we cannot be sure that the mechanical pursuit of desire will lead to socially beneficial outcomes. It is therefore necessary to ascertain the relative, contingent, and deliberated balance of the rights of individuals to and from the society in which they reside. Simultaneously, it is necessary to identify and balance the inherent tension within and between liberty and equality. To gain legitimacy and authority, this reasoning must be transparent, capable of review, and follow due process. Concomitantly, it is necessary to link the individual to communitarian underpinnings by exploring the relative role played by fairness (or, in a legal sense, principles of equity) and efficiency (normally, but not exclusively, calculated by cost considerations). This includes determining whether and how informed consent has been obtained and what sanctions could or should be imposed for breaking the written or unwritten principles governing the polity.

These core issues lie at the heart of the unfulfilled social contract imagined by Jean Jacques Rousseau. In lamenting the possibility of securing stability, he felt himself drawn to the politics of the strongman, as we are again today (Rousseau, 1968). Relegating the answer to a generic commitment to an apparently agreed non-calculative social contract overarching legal, governance, and transactional frameworks does little to resolve the underlying problem. A public philosophy integrating law and morality remains elusive, not least because of the decline in transcendent belief. In an increasingly secular age, we are witnessing a shift from what Taylor (2007, p. 713) calls 'hierarchical mediated-access societies to horizontal, direct access societies. And secondly, the modern social imaginary no longer sees the greater trans-local entities – nations, states, churches – as grounded in something other, something higher, than common action in secular time'. Paradoxically, this freedom, as Taylor (2007, p. 714) points out, may lead to disenchantment and nostalgia for the re-creation of some kind of order. None of this is to deny the moral value of identity but to situate it within a larger collective than used (and abused) in contemporary politics. The challenge is epitomized by the triumph of sloganeering. Pride can, however, come before a fall, especially when emotion trumps calculation in political games. When the winning hand appears to result only in the retention of the status quo, longer-term implications begin to emerge.

The Brexit bet displayed this chrematistic recklessness. Erroneously, it was viewed in tactical terms as a single transaction. There was little regard for either the long-term impact or the cost-benefit evaluation for the broader community. Issues like climate change make this much more difficult to quantify and evaluate. The launch into the unknown, fuelled only by hope, was one with little practical use or certainty. Running through all of this is the spectre of meaningless; that as a result of the denial of transcendence, of heroism, of deep feeling, we are left with a view of human life which is empty, cannot inspire commitment, offers nothing really worthwhile, cannot answer the craving for goals we can dedicate ourselves to. 'Human happiness can only inspire us when we have to fight against the forces which are destroying it; but once realised, it will inspire nothing but ennui, a cosmic yawn' (Taylor, 2007, p. 717).

What emerges when this normative backdrop is applied to the finance sector is how very particular and what a narrow form of culture and accompanying particularized logic it encapsulates. Culture and its commodification become part of the problem. This is socialized and given authority and standing according to self-referential but exclusive rather than inclusive terms. This occurs precisely because of the lack of an underpinning purpose or indeed philosophical grounding. The task is to design operational risk in a manner fit for purpose, a task that requires the redefinition of the purpose of banking in the first place. It is a fact acknowledged by the independent review into the culture of the British bank Barclays:

> Transforming the culture will require a new sense of purpose beyond the need to perform financially. It will require establishing shared values, supported by a code of conduct, that create a foundation for improving behaviours while accommodating the particular characteristics of the bank's different businesses. It will require a public commitment, with clear milestones and regular reporting on progress. It will require Barclays to listen to stakeholders, serve its customers and clients well and get on with the work to implement its plans and stay out of trouble. The complexity of Barclays' businesses makes this a particular challenge for its leaders. It will take time before it is clear that sustainable change is being achieved. (Salz, 2013, para. 2.20)

What should frame the interaction between law, morality, and social norms? This conundrum has animated discourse within legal and political philosophy across millennia. A narrow reading of liability may lead to a catastrophic loss in the court of public opinion in an age defined by anxiety and populist rage. The viral and boundless nature of social media increases the speed and deleterious capacity of informational flows on corporate reputation. It shortens decision-making time. It also strengthens the external antennae of participants with conflicting motives. Activists from across the stakeholder spectrum have differential interests in the outcome of individual battles within an existential conflict over the rights, duties, and responsibilities of the corporation. These activists include employees, suppliers, discontented shareholders representing disparate causes, the class action bar, and the increased scrutiny of (temporarily) empowered (if embattled) market-conduct regulators. Does accountability, on the other hand, lie in the acceptance of community expectations? Just what constitutes social expectation? Who should assess it and on what basis? Providing a framework to address these existential questions is the focus of the concluding section.

4 Withering on the Vine: The Future of the Corporation

The replacement of 'profit' as a proxy for efficiency with 'effectiveness' as a corporate or regulatory goal requires a granular definition of purpose.

Determining that purpose is far from uncontroversial or assured. For both the corporation and the state, it necessitates traversing what Acemoglu and Robinson (2019) term a 'narrow corridor' between coercion and benign neglect. When values conflict, as they necessarily do, which approach provides warranted trust in the trustworthiness of the corporate order? Should it derive from a contract imposed by legislative fiat or mandatory listing requirements? Alternatively, can enhanced voluntary disclosure of non-financial indicators of performance provide evidence of a functioning moral operating system?

Whichever approach is adopted, the rise of populism necessitates a fundamental recalibration of law and practice. This must, in turn, align internal risk management, external market and regulatory oversight, and community expectations. This recalibration requires a re-evaluation of the social and economic impacts of corporations. The analysis advanced here has applicability across sectors, most notably technology, the darling of unthinking disruption theorists. Questions over their oligopolistic tendencies and questionable stewardship over the security, use, and potential misuse of data has done much to undermine trust. In the contemporary world, the surveillance state is as much a corporate as a political one (Cohen, 2017). Given the changing nature of the fight against corruption, where algorithmic code control is as pernicious to electoral outcomes across the liberal order as in nascent democracies, no jurisdiction is immune; nor is there room for complacency.

Notwithstanding evidence to the contrary of its efficacy as a method of restraint, the shareholder primacy model (Fama & Jensen, 1983; Jensen & Meckling, 1976) retains a paradigmatic hold over legal and business research and corporate practice (Greenfield, 2006). On one level, this is unsurprising. Power, including that of academic status, once accreted, is rarely willingly ceded. At the same time, however, it is important to remember there is no, and never has been, legal justification for the assertion that the corporation exists for any other purpose than its long-term interests (Stout, 2007). The private ordering of the corporation and its governance is an ideational trope. It is not a natural ordering.

The corporation is a legal fiction. It has 'no body to kick, no soul to damn' (Nicol, 2018). Relatively unconstrained in temporal and spatial terms, it has the right to enter into contracts, to sue or be sued, to exercise freedom of speech, and contribute to political campaigns. In law, the corporation has legal personality. This begs an existential question: does the corporation owe duties and responsibilities to society, irrespective of where it is listed, domiciled, trades, or books profit and loss? If the answer is positive, what should be the role of regulation? On what normative basis should the activity of corporations be directed? These normative questions need answers.

The trifecta identified here – lack of internal and external control, failed deterrence and surveillance strategies, and loss of legitimacy – demonstrates the inextricable linkage between law and culture. Law offers a 'framework for ordered relationships' within society (Rosen, 2006, p. 7). Order is eroding through doubt in the trustworthiness of our institutions, including the corporation and those charged with its oversight (Rose, 2011; Mayer, 2019; O'Brien, 2019). Disbelief in corporate fealty to social obligation, particularly in the finance sector, contributes to the rise of populism and the undermining of public support for the liberal order itself (Deenan, 2018).

Unpacking the determinants of societal expectation to ascertain the 'validity' of the 'facticity' is far from an academic exercise (Habermas, 1996). It is critical to ongoing corporate and political legitimacy and authority, not least for the regulatory institutions that underpin its operation. Ascertaining rights, duties, and responsibilities was always, and continues to be, a contingent political calculation with uncertain outcomes. When faced with an existential threat on the scale of the Great Depression and resulting New Deal (O'Brien, 2014), or the 2008 global financial crisis and its aftermath, they can change dramatically (Deenan, 2018; Carney 2015; Kakutani, 2018; Kavanagh & Rich, 2018). The global COVID pandemic acts as an overlay to pre-existing conditions. Stability, even if uncertain, cannot be preserved by the presence of a Leviathan. Instead, transcending the warning of Thomas Hobbes (1985) requires 'a state that has the capacity to enforce laws, control violence, resolve conflicts, and provide services but is still tamed and controlled by an assertive, well-organised society . . . but building and defending – and controlling – a Shackled Leviathan takes effort, and is always a work in progress, often fraught with danger and instability' (Acemoglu & Robinson, 2019, pp. 24, 28). Stability and security require a renewed compromise in the perennial contestation between the market and the state, which reduces anxiety, provides security, and inculcates trust. Seen in this context, trust is a manifestation of a strong not a weak state (Acemoglu & Robinson, 2019, p. 72). It is only through constant and vigilant supervision that one can ensure the presence and maintenance of a believed and believable social contract.

Anthropologist Clifford Geertz identified the centrality of law to the construction of cultural practice. For Geertz (1996, p. 35), 'law doesn't just mop up. It defines. What it defines, the meaning frames it sets forth, is an important force in shaping human behaviour and giving it sense, lending it significance, point and direction'. For Geertz, these artificial constructs are essential. As he put it: 'man is an animal suspended in webs of significance he himself has spun, I take culture to be those webs, and the analysis of it to be therefore not an experimental science in search of law but an interpretive one in search of meaning'

(Geertz, 1973, p. 5). What is at issue then is not 'recourse to strict rules but on the maintenance of order through diverse social, economic and psychological pressures', because 'the meaning of a legal system's style of implementing moral propositions is incomprehensible without seeing its reverberations in other cultural contexts' (Rosen, 2006, pp. 26–8).

Regulatory theory is a pertinent example of such a complex web. Its integrative synthesis needs to be unspun in the search for meaning. Is the function and practice of regulation designed to achieve substantive change or, as long suspected (Edelman, 1964; Bell, 1976; Stone, 1975), does it merely provide the dramaturgical location for the elevation of symbolism through the construction of a political spectacle? Even its most influential progenitor (Landis, 1938) began to have his doubts by the end of his career (Landis, 1960). To begin answering this question necessitates mapping the complex, often unseen, interaction between power, politics, norms, vision, and law.

In metaphorical terms, regulatory politics is a marketplace of ideas where the legislative, regulatory, and 'soft law' norms that inform economic exchange are negotiated, often outside the judicial architecture (Porter & Ronit, 2006). It is only through exploration of the contractual nature of the exchange that the conscionability of the bargain between law and culture can be determined (Rosen, 2006, p. 9; Sandel, 2013). This requires an in-depth evaluation of how law is created (Hanrahan, 2018, pp. 11–12; O'Brien, 2019), not just its interpretation within and between communities of practice.

For the woman on the Clapham omnibus, the man on the Staten Island ferry, or the transgendered person on a Melbourne tram, there is no difference between unconscionable and unethical conduct. In law the distinction is pivotal. This is a very practical example of the function of ethical theory more generally, which is to 'describe the point, function, and limitations of rules' (Nussbaum, 2000, p. 59). This Element has distinguished between commitment to subjective, if sincerely held, 'values' and objective 'virtue'. This critical parsing is often lost in discussions of business ethics. Placing values at the centre of discourse (e.g., Gentiles, 2010) can give a patina of false legitimacy and lead to popular disillusion. Behind the Potemkin façade may be nothing of substance (or substantive difference but incommensurable moral equivalence). Ostensible strength in rhetorical terms may provide significant capacity to influence political and regulatory outcomes but allow for the triumph of sophistry over genuine ethical commitment.

There can be no doubting of the critical importance of the task. How to rebuild trust in distrusting times is one of the most existential questions facing contemporary society. We are approaching a *fin de siècle*. The challenge of populism has no single parentage. It can come from the right (United

States), the left (Greece and Spain), or have no discernible ethos beyond anger and resentment (France and Italy). Cynicism and the uncertain spread of the COVID pandemic are providing an accelerant. Each is being liberally doused upon the kindling of frustration, disenchantment, and disengagement. For the corporation, sovereign risk is equalling conduct and operational risk. Its own long-term interests, on which all corporate law theorists agree, rest on the corporation's survival. To do so, the core determinants that make up its culture must be delineated and evaluated holistically. What is required is substantive, not technical, compliance; warranted commitment to stated values; effective deterrence; enhanced accountability; and the development of risk-management systems appropriate to the profile of the organization itself.

This approach builds on an insight derived from Rossouw and van Vurren (2003). It places corporate responses to legal investigation within a continuum. One does not see linear progression based on a Pauline conversion. Instead, a strategic game is played. Calculation shifts according to political contingency. As Rossouw and van Vuuren make clear, no single corporation has a single culture. Rather, different subcultures coexist. Power is determined not only within the corporation itself but through cross-sector networks. The primary problem associated with financial services is one of miscalculating conduct risk. Elevating values, if compartmentalized rather than holistically deployed, can lead to relapse. Thus an amoral approach would see the corporation write off legal punishment in large part because the fine level and social opprobrium are so low. Similarly, a reactive corporation would adopt a minimal approach, not necessarily moving to identify systemic weaknesses and change cultural practices. At the third level, the focus is on developing compliance and risk-management systems consistent with industry best practice. The fourth level, that of integrity, would see voluntarily imposed enhancements. This leaves it to the corporation itself to decide commitments and then embed them in its constitution, making fealty a core fiduciary responsibility of the board, which cannot be delegated downwards.

This approach can be extended to the industry level through the enforceability of codes of conduct, the approach favoured by the Australian Royal Commission (2019, p. 112). The fifth and final approach – that of total alignment – would see active engagement with the state to deliver socially beneficial outcomes. The totally aligned model raises its own set of problems from a democratic perspective. This is particularly notable in an era of no caps on campaign contributions in the United States. Traces are also present in Australia in intervention in socially divisive issues, such as the same-sex referendum or the campaign for Aboriginal recognition in the Australian

Constitution. Those supportive of this intervention may have very different views on other issues, including, for example, climate change and energy policy.

The argument advanced here is that an integrity-based approach is not only the best available compromise, it is also the most sustainable and democratic option. Critically, it is not one that is included in existing contractual terms, which contributes to the current ineffectiveness of concluding litigation in the shadow of the state. This is not to suggest that it cannot be made more effective. In so doing, it would potentially provide a much greater demonstration effect than reliance on compliance alone, which is at the cornerstone of the three lines of defence, the contemporary dominant if discredited risk-management framework.

The three-lines model has the advantage of parsimony. It sacrifices accuracy in the search for generalizability. The simplicity is deceptive. It can be dangerous if misapplied. It works on the assumption that risk identification and management should be owned at the level of individual units. At the second line, risk and compliance policies and procedures act as internal gatekeepers. They perform a combined surveillance and guidance role. They operate as delegated agents with sub-principal power to control units and participants within them who are often responsible for setting remuneration. This inherent conflict of interest has rarely been managed well. The third line of defence is offered by internal and external audit. This provides assurance to the board that the system is working. However, if the risk is not identified, or deliberately obfuscated, the danger is obvious: the assurance is false. The cultural imperatives of the firm are either not cutting through the permafrost or the board is complicit. Either way, change is imperative and unavoidable. *The Royal Commission into Misconduct in the Banking, Superannuation and Financial Services Industry* (2019) is clear on this point.

> There remains a reluctance in some entities to form and then give practical effect to *their* understanding of what is ethical, of what is efficient, honest and *fair*, of what is the 'right' thing to do. Instead the entity contents itself with statements of purpose, vision, or values, too often expressed in terms that say little or nothing about those basis standards that underpin both the concept of misconduct and the community's standards and expectations. (Royal Commission, 2019, p. 412)

This leaves unresolved what those indicators could be or should be and how this can work in a holistic fashion consistent with independent review. When aligned to the fact that so few cases are litigated to a judicial conclusion, the weakness of contemporary risk systems and regulatory theory comes into clear view. Consistent with the core insight from hermeneutics, this Element provides an evidential basis 'to understand a complex whole from perceptions of its parts and their interrelationships' (Gadamer, 1976, p. 119).

The investigation has tested whether the prevailing consensus is the result of ideational factors that misconceive the very conception of liberalism they rely upon. Freedom is a morally neutral concept. It only gains traction and substance by how individual autonomy aligns with equality of opportunity. By taking and justifying through a strong evidential and theoretical base a contrarian stance to that consensus, the foundations of the existing paradigm begin to disintegrate. This allows for new knowledge and understanding to develop. In so doing, the research agenda proposed has real-world and academic impact on both corporate and regulatory practice. It thereby helps guide industry to the provision of socially beneficial outcomes through the operation of a renewed intergenerational social contract, notwithstanding the fact that such a contract is by its very nature fragile and unstable – and is likely to remain so. Ongoing vigilance is the price of freedom.

References

Acemoglu, D. & Robinson, J. (2019). *The Narrow Corridor*. London: Penguin Books.

Admati, A. (2017). It takes a village to maintain a dangerous financial system. In L. Herzog (ed.), *Just Financial Markets: Finance in a Just Society*. Oxford: Oxford University Press, pp. 293–321.

Agger, B. (1991). Critical theory, post-structuralism and postmodernism: Their sociological relevance. *Annual Review of Sociology*, 17, 105–31.

Agius. M. et al. (2010). Financial leaders pledge excellence and integrity. Letters to the editor, *Financial Times*, 29 September, www.ft.com/con tent/eb26484e-cb2d-11df-95c0-00144feab49a (accessed 5 November 2020).

Applebaum, B. (2019). *The Economists' Hour: False Prophets, Free Markets and the Fracture of Society*. New York: Little, Brown and Company.

Arendt, H. (2017). *The Origins of Totalitarianism*. London: Penguin Books.

Aristotle (2004a). *The Art of Rhetoric*. London: Penguin Classics.

(2004b). *The Nicomachean Ethics*. London: Penguin Classics.

Aronoff, K. (2017). Thank god it's Monday. *Dissent*, 64(1), 55–63.

Ashforth, B. & Anand, V. (2003). The normalization of corruption in organizations. *Research in Organizational Behavior*, 25, 1–52.

Audi, R. (2012). Virtue ethics as a resource in business. *Business Ethics Quarterly*, 22(2), 273–91.

(2004). *The Right in the Good: A Theory of Intuition and Intrinsic Value*. Princeton: Princeton University Press.

Augustine (2003). *City of God: Concerning the City of God against the Pagans*. London: Penguin Classics.

Ayres, I. & Braithwaite, J. (1992). *Responsive Regulation: Transcending and Deregulatory Debate*. Oxford: Clarendon Classics.

Barnard, C. (1938). *The Functions of the Executive*. Cambridge, MA: Harvard University Press.

Baron, J. & Bielby, W. (1980). Bringing the firms back in: Stratification, segmentation, and the organization of work. *American Sociological Review*, 45, 737–65.

Bell, D. (1976). *The Cultural Contradictions of Capitalism*. London: Heineman.

Benson, I. (2018) 'Values language': A cuckoo's egg or useful moral framework. In D. Daintree (ed.), *Creative Subversion: The Liberal Arts and Human Educational Fulfillment*. Brisbane: Connor Court, pp. 1–44.

Benson, M. & Simpson, S. (2015). *Understanding White Collar Crime: An Opportunity Perspective.* New York: Routledge.

Berle, A. (1960). Foreword. In E. Mason (ed.), *The Corporation in Modern Society.* Cambridge MA: Harvard University Press, pp. ix–xvi.

(1931). Corporate powers as powers in trust. *Harvard Law Review,* 44(7), 1049–74.

Berle, A. & Means, G. (1932). *The Modern Corporation and Private Property.* New York: Harcourt, Brace & World.

Bicchieri, C. (2016). *Norms in the Wild: How to Diagnose, Measure and Change Social Norms.* New York: Oxford University Press.

Biden, J. (2020). Why America must lead again. *Foreign Affairs,* 23 January, www.foreignaffairs.com/articles/united-states/2020–01-23/why-america-must-lead-again (accessed 3 February 2020).

Blair, M. & Stout, L. (1999). A team production theory of corporate law. *Virginia Law Review,* 85(2), 247–328.

Bommer, G. (2020). Expertise in research integration and implementation for tackling complex problems: When is it needed, where can it be found and how can it be strengthened? *Nature,* 6(5), www.nature.com/articles/s41599-019–0380-0.pdf (accessed 3 February 2020).

Bourdieu, P. (1996). *The State Nobility.* Cambridge: Polity.

(1990). *The Logic of Practice.* Stanford: Stanford University Press.

Bowie, N. & Freeman, R. (1992). *Ethics and Agency Theory.* New York: Oxford University Press.

Braithwaite, J. (2020). Regulatory mix, collective efficacy and crimes of the powerful. *Journal of White Collar and Corporate Crime,* 1(1), 62–71.

(2013). Cultures of redemptive finance. In J. O'Brien & G. Gilligan (eds.), *Integrity Risk and Accountability in Capital Markets: Regulating Culture.* Oxford: Hart Publishing.

Bratton, W. & Wachter, M. (2008). Shareholder primacy's corporatist origins: Adolf Berle and the modern corporation. *Journal of Corporation Law,* 34 (1), 99–152.

Brion, S., Mo, R. & Lount, R. (2018). Dynamic influences of power on trust: Changes in power affect trust in others. *Journal of Trust Research,* 9(1), 6–27.

Brown, G. (2009). Speech to G20 finance ministers. Speech delivered at the G2O Finance Ministers Meeting, St Andrews, Scotland, 7 November.

(2008). Introduction. In G. Himmelfarb, *The Roads to Modernity: The British, French and American Enlightenments.* London: Vintage.

Cardenas, J. C. & Ostrom, E. (2006). How norms help reduce the tragedy of the commons: A multi-layer framework for analysing field experiments. In

J. Drobak (ed.), *Norms and the Law*. New York: Cambridge University Press, pp. 105–38.

Carney, M. (2018, November 27). Letter to G20 leaders from FSB chair. *Financial Stability Board*, Buenos Aires.

(2017, March 21). Worthy of trust: Law, ethics and culture in banking. Speech delivered at the Bank of England Conference Centre, London.

(2015, September 21). Three truths for finance. Speech delivered at the Harvard Club UK, Southwark Cathedral, London.

(2014, May 27). Inclusive capitalism: Creating a sense of the systemic. Speech delivered at the Inclusive Capitalism Conference, London.

Chandler, A. (1977). *The Visible Hand: The Managerial Revolution in American Business*. Cambridge, MA: Harvard University Press.

Chiu, I-Y. (2015). *Regulating from the Inside: The Legal Framework for Internal Control in Banks and Financial Institutions*. Oxford: Hart Publishing.

Churchill, W. (1949, March 31). Speech delivered at MIT mid-century convocation. Massachusetts Institute of Technology, Cambridge, MA, www.winstonchurchill.org/resources/speeches/1946–1963-elder-statesman/mit-mid-century-convocation/ (accessed 12 February 2020).

Clegg, S. (2003). Managing organisation futures in a changing world of power/knowledge. In H. Tsoukas & C. Knudsen (eds.), *The Oxford Handbook of Organization Theory*. Oxford: Oxford University Press, pp. 536–67.

Clemens, E. (2009). The problem of the corporation: Liberalism and the large organization. In P. Adler (ed.), *The Oxford Handbook of Sociology and Organizational Studies*. Oxford: Oxford University Press, pp. 535–58.

Coffee, J. (2006). *Gatekeepers: The Professions and Corporate Governance*. Oxford: Oxford University Press.

Cohen, N. (2017). *The Know-It-Alls: The Rise of Silicon Valley as a Political Powerhouse and Social Wrecking Ball*. New York: Oneworld.

Collins, H. (1999). *Regulating Contracts*. Oxford: Oxford University Press.

Dahl, R. (1974). *Who Governs? Democracy and Power in an American City*. New Haven: Yale University Press.

(1957). The concept of power. *Behavioral Science*, 3(2), 201–15.

Dalrymple, W. (2019a, August 31). How a company builds an empire. *Financial Times*, L1–2.

(2019b). *The Anarchy: The Relentless Rise of the East India Company*. London: Bloomsbury.

Daly, H. & Cobb, J. (1994). *For the Common Good: Redirecting the Economy towards Community, the Environment, and a Sustainable Future*. Boston: Beacon Press.

Davies H. & Zhivitskaya, M. (2018). Three lines of defence: A robust organising framework, or just lines in the sand? *Global Policy*, 9(1), 34–42.

Davis, G. (2016). *The Vanishing American Corporation*. Oakland: Berret-Koehler.

(2009). *Managed by the Markets: How Finance Re-Shaped America*. Oxford: Oxford University Press.

Davis, G. & Zald, M. (2009). Sociological classics and the canon in the study of organizations. In P. Adler (ed.), *The Oxford Handbook of Sociology and Organizational Studies*. Oxford: Oxford University Press, pp.637–46.

Deenan, P. (2018). *Why Liberalism Failed*. New Haven: Yale University Press.

Denzau, A. & North, D. (1994). Shared mental models: Ideologies and institutions. *Kyklos*, 47(2), 3–31.

DiMaggio, P. & Powell, W. (1983). The iron cage revisited: Institutional isomorphism and collective rationality in organizational fields. *American Sociological Review*, 48, 147–60.

Dodd, E. M. (1932). For whom are corporate managers trustees. *Harvard Law Review*, 45(7), 1145–63.

Donaldson, T. & Dunfee, T. (1999). *Ties That Bind: A Social Contracts Approach to Business Ethics*. Boston: Harvard Business School Press.

Dryzck, J. (2012). *The Foundations of Deliberative Governance*. Oxford: Oxford University Press.

Du Guy, P. (2009). Max Weber and the ethics of office. In P. Adler (ed.), *The Oxford Handbook of Sociology and Organizational Studies*. Oxford: Oxford University Press, pp. 146–73.

Du Guy, P. & Vikkelsø, S. (2014). What makes organization? Organizational theory as a practical science. In P. Adler, P. Du Guy, G. Morgan & M. Reed (eds.), *The Oxford Handbook of Sociology, Social Theory, and Organization Studies: Contemporary Currents*. Oxford: Oxford University Press.

Eagleton, T. (2016). *Culture*. New Haven: Yale University Press.

Easterbrook, F. & Fischel, D. (1989). The corporate contract. *Columbia Law Review*, 89, 1416–48.

The Economist (2020, February 22). Big tech's $2trn bull run. Editorial, *The Economist*, 7.

Edelman, L. (2007). Overlapping fields and constructed legalities: The endogeneity of law. In J. O'Brien (ed.), *Private Equity, Corporate Governance and the Dynamics Of Capital Market Regulation*. London: World Scientific Press, pp. 53–88.

Edelman L. & Talesh, S. (2011). To comply or not to comply – that isn't the question: How business organizations construct the meaning of compliance. In C. Parker & V. Nielsen (eds.), *Explaining Compliance: Business Approaches to Regulation*. Cheltenham: Edward Elgar.

Edelman, M. (1964). *The Symbolic Uses of Politics*. Urbana: University of Illinois Press.

Edgecliffe-Johnson, A. & Platt, E. (2020, February 22). WeWork: How the ultimate unicorn deflated. Life and Arts. *Financial Times*, pp. 1–2.

Elliot, T. S. (1948). *Notes towards the Definition of a Culture*. London: Faber & Faber.

Etzioni, A. (1968). *The Active Society*. London: Collier-MacMillan.

Fama, E. & Jensen, M. (1983). Separation of ownership and control. *Law and Economics*, 26 (2), 301–25.

Fink, L. (2019). *Letter to CEOs: Purpose v. Profit*. New York: BlackRock Publications.

Fisch, J. (2013). The long road back: Business roundtable and the future of SEC rulemaking. *Seattle University Law Review*, 36, 695–730.

Fligstein, N. & Goldstein, A. (2015). The emergence of a finance culture in American households, 1989–2007. *Socio-Economic Review*, 13(3), 575–601.

Freedman, J. (1975). Crisis and legitimacy in the administrative process. *Stanford Law Review*, 27(4), 1041–76.

Freeman, R., Harris, J. & Zyglidopoulos, S. (2018). *Stakeholder Theory: Concepts and Strategies*. Cambridge: Cambridge University Press.

Friedland, R. & Alford, R. (1991). Bringing society back in: Symbols, practices and institutional contradictions. In W. Powell & P. DiMaggio (eds.), *The New Institutionalism in Organizational Analysis*. Chicago: Chicago University Press.

Friedman, M. (1970, September 13). The social responsibility of business is to increase its profits. *New York Times Magazine*, pp. 32–33, 122–26.

(1960). *Capitalism and Freedom*. Chicago: University of Chicago Press.

Foucault. M. (1995). *Discipline and Punish: The Birth of the Prison*. London: Vintage.

(1982). *The Archaeology of Knowledge: And the Discourse of Language*. London: Vintage.

Fuller, S. (2003). *Kuhn vs. Popper: The Struggle for the Soul of Science*. London: Icon Books.

Gadamer, H-G. (1976). *Philosophical Hermeneutics*. Berkeley: University of California Press.

(1975). *Truth and Method*. New York: Seasbury Press.

Gao, S. & Zhang, J. (2006). Stakeholder engagement, social auditing and corporate responsibility. *Business Process Management Journal*, 12(6), 722–40.

Geertz, C. (1973). *The Interpretation of Cultures*. New York: Basic Books.
  (1996). Off echoes: Some comments on anthropology and the law. *PoLAR*, 19 (2), 33–7.

Gentiles, M. (2010). *Giving Voice to Values: Vow to Speak Your Mind When You Know What Is Right*. New Haven: Yale University Press.

Glassman, C. (2002, September 27). Sarbanes-Oxley and the idea of 'good' governance. Speech delivered at the American Society of Corporate Secretaries, Washington, DC.

Gottschalk, P. (2017). *Organizational Opportunity and Deviant Behavior*. Northampton: Edward Elgar.

Gramsci, A. (1971). *Selections from the Prison Notebooks of Antonio Gramsci*. New York: International Publishers.

Greenfield, K. (2006). *The Failure of Corporate Law*. Chicago: University of Chicago Press.

Greenspan, A. (2008a, October 23). Evidence to the House Committee on Oversight and Government Reform, Washington, DC.
  (2008b, March 17). We will never have a perfect model of risk. *Financial Times*, 9.

Greenwood, R. & Miller, D. (2010). Tackling design anew: Getting back to the heart of organizational theory. *Academy of Management Perspectives*, 24 (4), 78–88.

Greve, H., Palmer, D. & Pozner, J-E. (2010). Organizations gone wild: The causes processes and consequences of organizational misconduct. *Academy of Management Annals*, 4(1), 53–107.

Gurria, A. (2017, June 6). *Globalization: Don't Patch It Up; Shake It Up*. Paris: OECD.

Habermas, J. (1996). *Between Facts and Norms: Contributions to a Discourse Theory of Law and Democracy*. Cambridge: Polity Press.
  (1981). *The Theory of Communicative Action: Reason and the Rationalization of Society*. Cambridge: Polity Press.

Halperin, J. L. (2011). Law in books and law in action: The problem of legal change. *Maine Law Review*, 64(1), 46–76.

Hancher, L. & Moran, M. (1989). Organizing regulatory space. In L. Hancher & M. Moran (eds.), *Capitalism, Culture and Economic Regulation*. Oxford: Oxford University Press.

Hanrahan, P. (2018). Legal framework for the provision of financial advice and sale of financial products to Australian households. *Royal Commission into*

Misconduct in the Banking, Superannuation and Financial Services Industry, Background Paper 7.

Hansmann, H. & Kraakman, R. (2001). The end of history for corporate law. *Georgetown Law Review*, 89, 439–668.

Hayek, F. (1943). *The Road to Serfdom*. London: Routledge.

Haywood, A. (1994). *Political Idea and Concepts: An Introduction*. London: MacMillan.

Hennis, W. (1988). *Max Weber: Essays in Reconstruction*. London: Allen & Unwin.

Hess, D. (2008). The three pillars of corporate social reporting as new governance reporting: Disclosure, dialogue and development. *Journal of Business Ethics*, 18(4), 447–82.

Himmelfarb, G. (2009). *The De-Moralization of Society: From Victorian Virtues to Modern Values*. London: IEA Health and Welfare Unit.

Hobbes, T. (1985). *Leviathan*. London: Penguin Classics.

Homans, G. (1964). Bringing the men back in. *American Sociological Review*, 29, 809–18.

Hood, C., Rothstein, H. & Baldwin, R. (2001). *The Government of Risk*. Oxford: Oxford University Press.

Ignatieff, M. (2017). *The Ordinary Virtues: Moral Order in a Divided World*. Cambridge, MA: Harvard University Press.

Ireland, P. (2000). Defending the rentier: Corporate theory and the reprivatisation of the public company. In J. Parkinson, A. Gamble & G. Kelly (eds.), *The Political Economy of the Company*. Oxford: Hart Publishing, pp. 141–74.

Jensen, M. & Meckling, W. (1976). Theory of the firm: Managerial behaviour, agency costs and ownership structure. *Journal of Financial Economics*, 3(4), 305–60.

Johnson, P. (2010). *Making the Market: The Victorian Origins of Corporate Capitalism*. Cambridge: Cambridge University Press.

Kakutani, M. (2018). *The Death of Truth*. London: Harper Collins.

Kaptein, M. (2008). Developing and testing a measure for the ethical culture of organizations: The corporate ethical virtues model. *Journal of Organizational Behavior*, 29(7), 923–47.

Karsgaard, M. A., Kautz, J., Bliese, P., Samson, K. & Kostyszyn, P. (2018). Conceptualizing time as a level of analysis: New directions in the analysis of trust dynamics. *Journal of Trust Research* 8(2), 142–65.

Kavanagh, J. & Rich, M. (2018). *Truth Decay: An Initial Exploration of the Diminishing Role of Facts and Analysis in American Public Life*. Santa Monica, CA: Rand Corporation.

Klein, H. & Myers, M. (1999). A set of principles for conducting and evaluating interpretative field studies in information systems. *MIS Quarterly*, 23(1), 67–94.

Klenowski, P. (2012). 'Learning the good with the bad': Are occupational white-collar offenders taught to neutralize their crimes? *Criminal Justice Review*, 37(4), 461–77.

Kornrich, S. & Hicks, A. (2015). The rise of finance: Causes and consequences of financialization. *Socio-Economic Review*, 13(3), 411–15.

Kuhn, T. (1962). *The Structure of Scientific Revolutions*. Chicago: University of Chicago Press.

Landis, J. (1960, December). Report on regulatory agencies to the president-elect. Washington, DC.

(1938). *The Administrative Process*. New Haven: Yale University Press.

(1931). The study of legislation in law schools. *Harvard Graduates' Magazine*, 39, 433–40.

Lazarus, R. (2009). Super-wicked problems and climate change: Restraining the present to liberate the future. *Cornell Law Review*, 94, 1115–1233.

Leclercq-Vandelannoitte, A. & Isaac, H. (2016). The new office: How cow-orking changes the work concept. *Journal of Business Strategy*, 37(6), 3–9.

Lessig, L. (2018). *America Compromised*. Chicago: University of Chicago Press.

Levin, K., Cashore, S. & Auld, G. (2012). Overcoming the tragedy of super-wicked problems: Constraining our future selves to ameliorate global climate change. *Policy Sciences*, 45(2), 121–52.

Lindblom, C. (1977). *Politics and Markets*. New York: Basic Books.

Luhmann, N. (1979). *Trust and Power*. Chichester: John Wiley & Sons.

Lukes, S. (1974). *Power: A Radical View*. London: Macmillan.

Lumineau, F. & Schilke, O. (2018). Trust development across levels of analysis: An embedded-agency perspective. *Journal of Trust Research*, 8(2), 238–48.

MacGillis, A. (2019, November 18). After the crash. *The New Yorker*, pp. 51–61.

MacIntyre, A. (1999). Social structures and their threat to moral agency. *Philosophy*, 74(3), 311–29.

(1984). *After Virtue*. South Bend: University of Notre Dame Press.

MacKenzie, D. (2009). *Material Markets: How Economic Agents Are Constructed*. Oxford: Oxford University Press.

MacNeil, I. & O'Brien, J. (2010). *The Future of Financial Regulation*. Oxford: Hart Publishing.

Macpherson, C. (1985). Introduction. In T. Hobbes, *Leviathan*. London: Penguin Classics, pp. 9–64.

Mallaby, S. (2019, September). How economists' faith in markets broke America. *The Atlantic*, www.theatlantic.com/magazine/archive/2019/09/nicolas-lemann-binyamin-appelbaum-economics/594718/ (accessed 12 February 2020).

Mann, M. (1986). *The Sources of Social Power*. Cambridge: Cambridge University Press.

Mason, E. (1960). Introduction. In E. Mason (ed.), *The Corporation in Modern Society*. Cambridge, MA: Harvard University Press.

(1958). The apologetics of managerialism. *Journal of Business*, 31(1), 1–11.

Mather, L. (2013). Law and society. In K. Whittington, R. Kelemen, & G. Caldeira (eds.), *The Oxford Handbook of Law and Politics*. Oxford: Oxford University Press, pp. 681–97.

Mayer, C. (2019). *Prosperity: Better Business Makes the Greater Good*. Oxford: Oxford University Press.

McBarnet, D. (2010). Financial engineering or legal engineering? Legal work, legal integrity, and the banking crisis. In I. MacNeil & J. O'Brien (eds.), *The Future of Financial Regulation*. Oxford: Hart Publishing, pp. 67–82.

McBarnet, D. & Whelan, C. (1999). *Creative Accounting and the Cross-Eyed Javelin Thrower*. Chichester: John Wiley & Sons.

Medcraft, G. (2019, April 11). Panel discussion on the Human Centred Business Model, IMF/World Bank spring meeting, Washington, DC.

Mill, J. S. [1859] (2006). *On Liberty and the Subjugation of Women*. London: Penguin Classics.

Miller. S. (2017). *Institutional Corruption: A Study in Applied Philosophy*. Cambridge: Cambridge University Press.

(2010). *The Moral Foundations of Social Institutions: A Philosophical Study*. Cambridge: Cambridge University Press.

Mills, C. (1956). *The Power Elite*. New York: Oxford University Press.

Mintzberg, H. (1983). *Power in and around Organizations*. Englewood Cliffs: Prentice Hall.

Mitroff, I. & Pearson, C. (1993). *Crisis Management: A Diagnostic Guide for Preparing Your Organization's Crisis Preparedness*. San Francisco: Jossey-Bass.

Moore, D., Tetlock, P., Tanlu, L. & Bazerman, M. (2006). Conflicts of interest and the case of auditor independence: Moral seduction and strategic issue cycling. *Academy of Management Review*, 31(1), 10–29.

Moore, G. (2012). The virtue of governance, the governance of virtue. *Business Ethics Quarterly*, 22(2), 293–318.

Moorhead, R., Vaughan, S. & Godinho, C. (2018). *In-House Lawyers' Ethics: Institutional Logics, Legal Risk and the Tournament of Influence*. Oxford: Hart Publishing.

Morgan, G. (1986). *Images of Organisation*. Thousand Oaks, CA: Sage.

Morse, J. (1999). Who is the ethics expert? The original footnote to Plato. *Business Ethics Quarterly*, 9(4), 693–7.

Mudrack, P. & Mason, E. (2019). Utilitarian traits and the Janus-headed model: Origins, meaning, and interpretation. *Journal of Business Ethics*, 156(2), 227–40.

Muller, J. (2016). *What Is Populism?* Philadelphia: University of Pennsylvania Press.

Munir, K. (2011). Financial crisis 2008–2009: What does the silence of institutional theorists tell us? *Journal of Management Inquiry*, 20, 114–17.

Murdoch, I. ([1960], 1999). *The Sovereignty of Good*. London: Routledge.

Murphy, H. (2020, February 19). Facebook accused of downplaying IP value in $9bn tax case. *Irish Times*, www.irishtimes.com/business/economy/facebook-accused-of-downplaying-ip-value-in-9bn-us-tax-case-1.4178362 (accessed 21 February 2020).

Myers, M. & Klein, H. (2011). A set of principles for conducting critical research in information systems. *MIS Quarterly*, 35(1), 17–36.

Nadar, R., Green, M. & Seligman, J. (1976). *Taming the Giant Corporation*. New York: W. H. Norton & Co.

Nicol, N. (2018). No body to kick, no soul to damn: Responsibility and accountability for the financial crisis (2007–2010). *Journal of Business Ethics*, 15(1), 101–14.

Nichols, T. (2017). *The Death of Expertise: The Campaign against Established Knowledge and Why It Matters*. New York: Oxford University Press.

Nielsen, R. (2003). Organizational theory and ethics: Varieties and dynamics of constrained optimisation. In H. Tsoukas & C. Knudsen (eds.), *The Oxford Handbook of Organization Theory*. Oxford: Oxford University Press, pp. 476–501.

Nietzsche, F. (2013). *On the Genealogy of Morals*. London: Penguin Classics.

Noordegraff, M. (2019). Weaknesses of wickedness: A critical perspective on wickedness theory. *Policy and Society*, 38(2), 278–97.

North, D. (1990). *Institutions, Institutional Change and Economic Performance*. New York: Cambridge University Press.

(1981). *Structure and Change in Economic History*. New York: Cambridge University Press.

Nussbaum, M. (2000). Why practice needs ethical theory: Particularism, principle and bad behavior. In S. Burton (ed.), *The Path of Law and Its Influence: The Legacy of Oliver Wendell Holmes Jnr.* New York: Cambridge University Press, pp. 50–86.

Obama, B. (2009, June 17). Remarks by the President on 21st-century financial regulatory reform. Speech delivered at Press Conference, White House, Washington, DC.

O'Brien, J. (2020). The moral foundations of stakeholder capitalism. *Law and Financial Markets Review*, 14(1), 1–4.

(2019). *Trust, Accountability and Purpose: The Regulation of Corporate Governance*. Cambridge: Cambridge University Press.

(2014). *The Triumph, Tragedy and Lost Legacy of James M Landis*. Oxford: Hart Publishing.

(2013). The facade of enforcement: Goldman Sachs, negotiated prosecution, and the politics of blame. In S. Will, D. Brotherton, & S. Handelman (eds.), *How They Got Away with It: Lessons from the Financial Meltdown*. New York: Columbia University Press.

(2010). The future of financial regulation: Embedding integrity through design. *Sydney Law Review*, 32, 63–85.

(2009). *Engineering a Financial Bloodbath*. London: Imperial College Press.

(2007). *Redesigning Financial Regulation*. Chichester: John Wiley & Sons.

(2003). *Wall Street on Trial*. Chichester: John Wiley & Sons.

O'Brien, J. & Gilligan, G. (2013). *Integrity, Risk and Accountability in Capital Markets: Regulating Culture*. Oxford: Hart Publishing.

O'Neill, J. (2019). No more nice Dems. *New York Review of Books*, December, pp. 91–4.

Parfit, D. (2011). *On What Matters*. Oxford: Oxford University Press.

Parliamentary Commission on Banking Standards (2013). *Changing Banking for Good*. London: The Stationary Office.

Patriotta, G. & Starkey, K. (2008). From utilitarian morality to moral imagination: Reimagining the business school. *Journal of Management Inquiry* 17(4), 319–27.

Peters, B. G. (2017). What is wicked about wicked problems: A conceptual analysis and a research program. *Policy and Society*, 36(3), 385–96.

Piketty, T. (2020). *Capitalism and Ideology*. Cambridge, MA: Belknap Press.

(2018). *Brahmin left vs merchant right: Rising inequality and the changing structure of political conflict: Evidence from France, Britain, and the US, 1948–1970*. World Inequality Database, Working Paper 2018/7, March.

(2017). *Capital in the Twenty-First Century*. Cambridge, MA: Harvard University Press.

Pistor, K. (2020). *The Code of Capital*. Trenton: Princeton University Press.

Poggi, G. (2001). *Forms of Power*. Cambridge: Polity Press.

Polanyi, K. (1944). *The Great Transformation: The Political and Economic Origins of Our Time*. New York: Farrar & Reinhart.

Popper, K. [1945] (1984). *The Open Society and Its Enemies. Volume 2: Hegel and Marx*. London: Routledge.

(1959). *The Logic of Scientific Discovery*. London: Hutchinson.

Porter, T. & Ronit, K. (2006). Self-regulation as policy process: The multiple and criss-crossing stages of private rule making. *Policy Sciences*, 39(1), 41–72.

Pound, R. (1910). Law in books and law in action. *American Law Review*, 44(1), 12–36.

Raffnsøe, S. (2013). Beyond rule: Trust and power as capacities. *Journal of Political Power*, 6(2), 241–60.

Rahim, M. & Idowu, S. (eds.). (2015). *Social Audit Regulation: Development, Challenges and Opportunities*. Heidelberg: Springer International.

Rakoff, J. (2019). The problematic American experience with deferred prosecution agreements. *Law and Financial Markets Review*, 13(1), 1–3.

(2014, January 9). The financial crisis: Why have so few high-level executives been punished. *New York Review of Books*, www.nybooks.com/articles/2014/01/09/financial-crisis-why-no-executive-prosecutions/.

Rand, A. (1957). *Atlas Shrugged*. New York: Random House.

Rittel, H. & Webber, M. (1973). Dilemmas in a general theory of planning. *Policy Sciences*, 4(2), 155–69.

Roberts, N. (2000). Wicked problems and network approaches to resolution. *International Public Management Review*, 1(1), 1–19.

Rose, D. (2011). *The Moral Foundations of Economic Behavior*. New York: Oxford University Press.

Rosen, J. (2017). *Louis D. Brandeis: American Prophet*. New Haven: Yale University Press.

Rosen, L. (2006). *Law as Culture*. Princeton: Princeton University Press.

Ross, E. A. (1907). *Sin and Society*. Boston: Houghton Mifflin.

Ross, W. D. (1930). *The Right and the Good*. Oxford: Oxford University Press.

Rousseau, D., Stikin, S., Burt, R. & Camerer, C. (1998). Not so different after all: Across-discipline view of trust. *Academy of Management Review*, 23 (3), 393–404.

Rousseau, J. J. (1968). *The Social Contract*. London: Penguin Classics.

Rossouw, G. & van Vurren, L. (2003). Modes of managing morality: A descriptive model of modes of managing ethics. *Journal of Business Ethics*, 46(4), 389–402.

Rothschild, E. (1994). Adam Smith and the invisible hand. *American Economic Review*, 84(2), 319–22.

Royal Commission into Misconduct in the Banking, Superannuation and Financial Services Industry (2019, November). Final report. Canberra: Commonwealth of Australia.

(2018, November). *Interim report*. Canberra: Commonwealth of Australia.

Rumsfeld, D. (2002, February 12). Secretary of Defense news briefing. Washington, DC, Department of Defense.

Salz, A. (2103, April). An independent review of Barclays business practices. Barclays Banks, www.online.wsj.com/public/resources/documents/SalzReview04032013.pdf (accessed 10 February 2020).

Sandel, M. (2013). *What Money Can't Buy: The Moral Limits of Markets*. New York: Farrar, Strauss & Giroux.

Schumpeter, J. (1943). *Capitalism, Socialism and Democracy*. New York: Harper & Row.

Seneca. (2004). *Letters from a Stoic*. London: Penguin Classics.

Sennett, R. (1998). *The Corrosion of Character: The Personal Consequence of Work in the New Capitalism*. New York: W. W. Norton & Co.

Shipolov, A. & Gawer, A. (2020). Integrating research on interorganizational networks and ecosystems. *Academy of Management Annals*, 14(1), 92–121.

Skocpol, T. (1985). Bring the state back in: Strategies of analysis in current research. In P. Evans, D. Rueschemeyer, & T. Skcpol (eds.), *Bringing the State Back In*. Cambridge: Cambridge University Press.

Smircich, L. (1983). Concepts of culture and organizational analysis. *Administrative Science Quarterly* 28(3), 339–58

Smith, A. [1759] (2006). *The Theory of Moral Sentiments*. Minuela: Dover Books.

[1776] (2005). *The Wealth of Nations*. London: Penguin.

Somers, M. & Block, F. (2014a). *The Power of Market Fundamentalism: Karl Polanyi's Critique*. Cambridge, MA: Harvard University Press.

(2014b). The return of Karl Polyani. *Dissent*, 61(2), 30–33.

Stadler, W. & Benson, M. (2012). Revisiting the guilty mind. *Criminal Justice Review*, 37(4), 494–511.

Stahl, B. S. (2004). Interpretative accounts and fairy tales: A critical polemic against the empiricist bias in interpretative research. *European Journal of Information Systems*, 23(1), 1–11.

Starbuck, W. & Milliken, F. (1998). Challenger: Fine-tuning the odds until something breaks. *Journal of Management Studies*, 25, 319–40.

Steiner, G. (1971). *In Bluebeards Castle: Some Notes towards the Redefinition of Culture*. London: Faber & Faber.

Stinchcombe, A. (1982). Should sociologists forget their mothers and fathers? *American Sociologist*, 17, 2–11.

Stone, C. (1975). *Where the Law Ends: The Social Control of Corporate Behaviour*. New York: Harper & Row.

Stout, L. (2019). Corporations as sempiternal legal persons. In T. Clarke, J. O'Brien, & C. O'Kelley (eds.), *The Oxford Handbook of the Corporation*. Oxford: Oxford University Press, pp. 220–33.

(2007). The mythical benefits of shareholder value. *Virginia Law Review*, 93 (3), 789–809.

(2006). Social norms and other-regarding preferences. In J. Drobak (ed.), *Norms and the Law*. New York: Cambridge University Press.

Streeck, W. (2016), *How Will Capitalism End? Essays on a Failing System*. London: Verso.

Sutherland, E. (1939). White-collar criminality. *American Sociological Review*, 5(1), 1–12.

Taylor, C. (2007). *A Secular Age*. Boston: Belknap Press.

Termeer, C., Dewulf, A. & Biesbroek, R. (2019). A critical assessment of the wicked problem concept: Relevance and usefulness for policy science and practice. *Policy and Society*, 38(2), 165–79.

Thornton, P. (2009). The value of the classics. In P. Adler (ed.), *The Oxford Handbook of Sociology and Organizational Studies*. Oxford: Oxford University Press, pp. 20–36.

(1999). The sociology of entrepreneurship. *Annual Review of Sociology*, 25, 19–46.

Van der Zwan, N. (2014). Making sense of financialization. *Socio-Economic Review*, 12(1), 99–129.

Vinten, G. (1990). The social auditor. *International Journal of Value-Based Management*, 3(2), 125–35.

Walsham, D. (2006). Doing interpretative research. *European Journal of Information Systems*, 15, 320–30.

(1993). *Interpreting Information Systems in Organisations*. Chichester: John Wiley & Sons.

Weaver, G. (2001). Ethics programs in global businesses: Culture's role in managing ethics. *Journal of Business Ethics*, 30(1), 3–15.

Weber, M. (1958). *The Protestant Ethic and the Spirit of Capitalism*. New York: Scribner.

(1994). The profession and vocation of politics. In P. Lassman & R. Speirs (eds.), *Weber: Political Writings*. Cambridge: Cambridge University Press.

Weick, K. (2009). Theory and practice in the real world. In H. Tsoukas & C. Knudsen (eds.), *The Oxford Handbook of Organization Theory*. Oxford: Oxford University Press, pp. 453–75.

(1995). *Sensemaking in Organizations*. Thousand Oaks, CA: Sage.

(1988). Enacted sensemaking in crisis situations. *Journal of Management Studies*, 25(4), 305–17.

Weick, K. & Sutcliffe, K. (2015). *Managing the Unexpected: Sustained Performance in a Complex World*. San Francisco: Jossey Bass.

Weick, K., Sutcliffe, K. & Obstfeld, F. (2005). Organizing and the process of sensemaking. *Organization Science*, 16(4), 409–21.

Williamson, O. (1996). *The Mechanisms of Governance*. New York: Oxford University Press.

(2000). The new institutional economics: Taking stock, looking ahead. *Journal of Economic Literature*, 38(3), 596–613.

Winter, M. (2019). *All Politics Is Local: Why Progressives Must Fight for the States*. New York: Bold Type.

Žižek, S. (2019). *Like a Thief in Broad Daylight: Power in the Era of Post-Humanity*. London: Penguin.

(2017). *The Courage of Hopelessness: Chronicles of a Year of Living Dangerously*. London: Allen Lane.

Acknowledgements

This work is a counterpart to *Trust, Accountability and Purpose: The Regulation of Corporate Governance* (2019), published in the Elements in Corporate Governance series. It is built on just under two decades of work on financial scandal, which has seen me amass more air miles and status credits than wise. It also allowed for the creation of a network that still provides essential intellectual and emotional nourishment, support and, as importantly, laughter. With everyone grounded, literally, we are forced to interact virtually. My thanks to David Chaike, Juliette Overland, and Gail Pearson at the University of Sydney for making me feel so welcome, and Pamela Hanrahan (UNSW), and Andy Schmulow (University of Wollongong), who have remained steadfast in their support. Claire Armstrong performed an amazing job copyediting the text, while Susan pushed me to be the best that I could be. I am grateful to the Australian Research Council for funding a major Discovery Grant, *Regulatory Power and Corporate Misconduct* (2019–21), on which I work alongside Ian Ramsay (University of Melbourne). I am, as always, indebted to my friends and family. My eldest brother Brian died in October as this Element was going to press. It is a devastating loss for the family. We will all miss him very much and it is fitting that this Element is dedicated to his memory. My elder brothers, Kieran and TJ, shouldered the responsibility of the funeral with great grace and dignity. I will always be grateful to them and to my son Justin, who stepped in to represent me. His public speaking skills were apparent in reading the liturgy at the funeral mass, something we all were exceptionally proud of, including, no doubt, Brian himself.

Cambridge Elements $\equiv$

Organization Theory

Nelson Phillips
Imperial College London
Nelson Phillips is the Abu Dhabi Chamber Professor of Strategy and Innovation at Imperial College London. His research interests include organization theory, technology strategy, innovation, and entrepreneurship, often studied from an institutional theory perspective.

Royston Greenwood
University of Alberta
Royston Greenwood is the Telus Professor of Strategic Management at the University of Alberta, a Visiting Professor at the University of Cambridge, and a Visiting Professor at the University of Edinburgh. His research interests include organizational change and professional misconduct.

Advisory Board

About the Series

Organization theory covers many different approaches to understanding organizations. Its focus is on what constitutes the how and why of organizations and organizing, bringing understanding of organizations in a holistic way. The purpose of *Elements in Organization Theory* is to systematize and contribute to our understanding of organizations.

Cambridge Elements $\equiv$

Organization Theory

Elements in the Series

A full series listing is available at: www.cambridge.org/EORT

Printed in the United States
by Baker & Taylor Publisher Services